M000315353

FLYING WARBIRDS

AN ILLUSTRATED PROFILE OF
THE FLYING HERITAGE COLLECTION'S
RARE WWII-ERA AIRCRAFT

CORY GRAFF

ZENITH PRESS

First published in 2014 by Zenith Press, an imprint of Quarto Publishing Group USA Inc., 400 First Avenue North, Suite 400, Minneapolis, MN 55401 USA

Zenith Press titles are also available at discounts in bulk quantity for industrial or sales-promotional use. For details write to Special Sales Manager at Quarto Publishing Group USA Inc., 400 First Avenue North, Suite 400, Minneapolis, MN 55401 USA.

To find out more about our books, visit us online at www.zenithpress.com.

Library of Congress Cataloging-in-Publication Data
Graff, Cory, 1971-
  Flying warbirds : an illustrated profile of the Flying Heritage Collection's rare WWII-era aircraft / Cory Graff.
    pages cm
  Includes index.
  ISBN 978-0-7603-4649-5 (hbk.)
  1. Airplanes, Military—History—20th century. 2. Flying Heritage Collection. 3. World War, 1939-1945—Aerial operations. I. Title.
II. Title: Illustrated profile of the Flying Heritage Collection's rare WWII-era aircraft.
  UG1240.G63 2014
  940.54'407479771--dc23
                    2014023124

Acquisitions Editor: Erik Gilg
Design Managers: James Kegley and Rebecca Pagel
Cover Designer: Kent Jenson
Designer: Simon Larkin
Layout: Rebecca Pagel

Printed in China

10 9 8 7 6 5 4 3 2 1

Cover photo: The FHC's North American P-51D Mustang is one of the most accurately restored World War II fighters in the world. *Jim Larsen*

Overleaf: The Republic P-47D Thunderbolt, with its big barrel-shaped nose, was lovingly called the "Jug" by pilots. *Heath Moffatt Photography*

Back cover photo: The FHC's main hangar was constructed by Alaska Airlines after World War II. The vintage building is the perfect venue to display some of the rarest aircraft in the world. *Flying Heritage Collection*

Frontispiece: The FHC's Supermarine Spitfire. *Jim Larson*

Title pages: After a day of flying, the aircraft are put away and staffers prepare to close the FHC's hangar doors. *Flying Heritage Collection*

CONTENTS

PREFACE

THE FLYING HERITAGE COLLECTION

The Puget Sound region is one of the hotbeds of American aviation. In 1916, William Boeing flew his first airplane from the waters of Lake Union near downtown Seattle. During World War II, thousands of B-17 and B-29 heavy bombers were built in Seattle and Renton, and the era of the jumbo jet began when the first Boeing 747 took to the skies from Paine Field near Everett, Washington, in 1969.

Boeing's factory at Paine Field is the largest building in the world by volume: New airliners emerge from this facility each day, winging away to all parts of the globe. The Flying Heritage Collection (FHC) moved to Paine Field from a small group of hangars in Arlington, Washington, in June 2008.

The FHC is unique. Established by philanthropist and Microsoft Corporation co-founder Paul G. Allen, it provides the vehicle for Allen to share his private collection of rare aircraft and artifacts with the public. The FHC is operated by Friends of Flying Heritage, a 501(c)(3) non-profit organization.

The collection focuses on technical themes from an era of amazingly rapid change. The concept of changes in technology—as seen through the aircraft, artifacts, and their surrounding exhibits—was a natural fit for Allen, a pioneer in the fields of computer software systems and industrial science.

Allen was also influenced by the experiences of his father, who joined the US Army and served in Europe during World War II. Kenneth Allen landed at Normandy in June

LEFT: When American air power had taken over European skies, many US warplanes left the factory without camouflage. The bare metal airplanes were faster and lighter, and they could be accepted by the army a few days sooner. Both the FHC's P-51 and P-47 fly without camouflage.

1944 and moved through France, Belgium, and Germany during the last year of that conflict. Undoubtedly, the stories he told young Paul upon his return planted the seed of interest in World War II history.

The FHC operates from a pair of hangars on the south end of Paine Field's nearly two-mile-long main runway. The primary hangar was constructed after World War II for the repair and maintenance of Alaska Airlines passenger planes. However, due to the Korean War and Cold War needs, the big hangar was quickly turned over to the US Air Force. Today, it serves as an excellent place to display and maintain the aircraft in the collection.

Two aspects set the FHC apart from other aviation museums and flying collections. First, the aircraft are restored

immaculately. Each airplane looks as it did when it rolled out of the factory or when it was serving with an operational squadron during the war. The FHC staff is dedicated to restoring and maintaining the aircraft as accurately as possible. An example of this can be seen in the mechanic's shop where drawers of hardware line the walls. Even for something as simple as a common bolt, there are different fasteners for each nation's aircraft—from the Spitfire (British Imperial), to the Mustang (US government AN), to the Bf 109 (German metric).

An aircraft like the B-25J gives another demonstration of the FHC's dedication to accuracy. While many flying Mitchells are bare on the interior, so patrons can be sold rides, the FHC aircraft contains a full complement of wartime equipment. Hauling thousands of pounds of weaponry, survival equipment, and communications gear may slow the plane and burn additional fuel, but it more accurately demonstrates the character and capabilities of this wartime medium bomber.

BELOW: The FHC often hosts visiting vintage aircraft during the peak months. Here, the collection's P-51 Mustang and Commemorative Air Force Boeing B-17G *Sentimental Journey* share the ramp at the start of a day of flying.

Secondly, most aircraft in the FHC are restored to flyable condition. Many air museums are static institutions. One might ask, "If you wanted to know about a fox, would you go and stare at one on the shelf of a taxidermist's shop?" The best way to experience the animal is in its natural habitat. In the case of a vintage fighter plane, its natural habitat is the sky.

At the FHC, visitors can not only see, but hear, smell, and feel these magnificent machines from decades past. Nothing compares to hearing the growl of the Spitfire's Rolls-Royce engine, seeing the *Storch* nearly hover in the face of a headwind, or watching the Hellcat go thundering past, hot on the tail of a Zero fighter.

In order to "keep 'em flying," the FHC hangars contain work areas, as well as display spaces. A staff of five full-time mechanics keeps these planes in top flying shape. In the summer, the mechanics are prepping the planes for flight and, in the winter, they are tearing them down and inspecting every part.

In the open hangar, mechanics jack up the planes to test their landing gear, delve into the inner workings of their engines, change brakes, and troubleshoot radios. Periodically, they take an aircraft outside the hangar doors, tie it down, and rattle the windows with a noisy engine run.

The planes fly locally and perform regularly at Paine Field, as well as visit air shows in western Washington. From May to September, the FHC holds free Fly Days at its home base. Commonly, two or more aircraft fly—for example, the Spitfire and Hurricane on Battle of Britain Day, or the Bf 109 and Fw 190 on Luftwaffe Day. Some weekends, the lucky crowd is treated to a performance starring the only flying example of that aircraft left in the world.

continued on page 14

BELOW: On warm summer days, visitors can watch the maintenance activities happening right outside the FHC's hangar doors. To see one of these iconic airplanes is one thing. To hear it roar to life, smell the oily exhaust, and to feel the powerful engine rumble in your chest, is quite another experience!

ABOVE: The Soviet T-34/85 medium tank was designed as the answer to the large and powerful German tanks encountered on the Eastern Front. The FHC's example was built from an armored recovery vehicle found in Czechoslovakia.

ABOVE: The trusty M4A1 Sherman was the primary weapon of the US Army tank corps during World War II. The FHC's example was built in Chicago, served as a training tool in the United States, and was sent to the Dutch army after the war. After it was abandoned, the tank was fully restored in England.

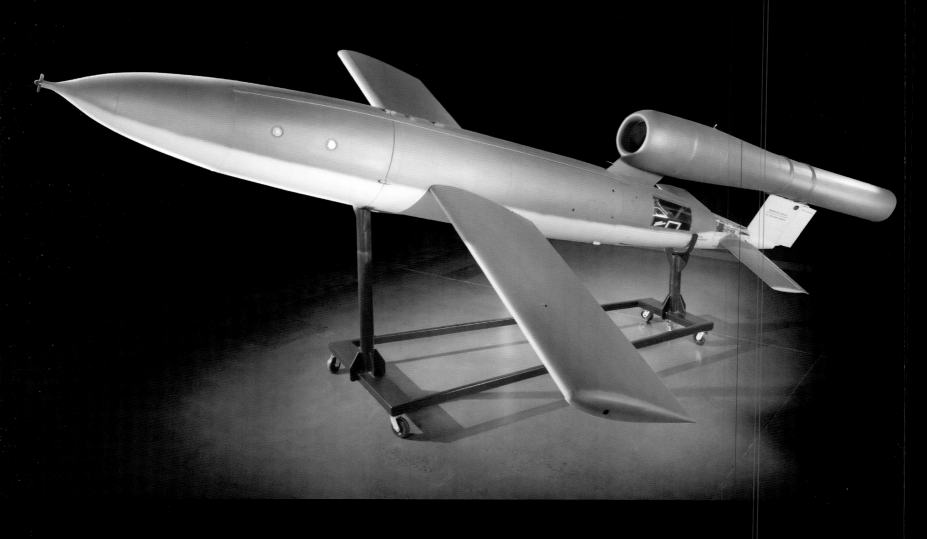

RIGHT: The fearsome V-2 rocket was the first manmade object to go into space. Some of the technologies developed for this Nazi "vengeance weapon" helped launch men to the moon some twenty-five years later.

BELOW: Germany's 88mm flak gun was developed in secret after World War I. Though built for anti-aircraft duties, soldiers found that it would do terrible damage when aimed at a vehicle or pillbox. By World War II, it was one of the weapons feared most by Allied troops and pilots.

OPPOSITE, BELOW: The FHC's V-1 "Buzz Bomb" is an example of the world's first cruise missile. Loaded with explosives, the pulse-jet powered machines came down in London during World War II. The parts to make the FHC's example came from an underground factory near Nordhausen, Germany.

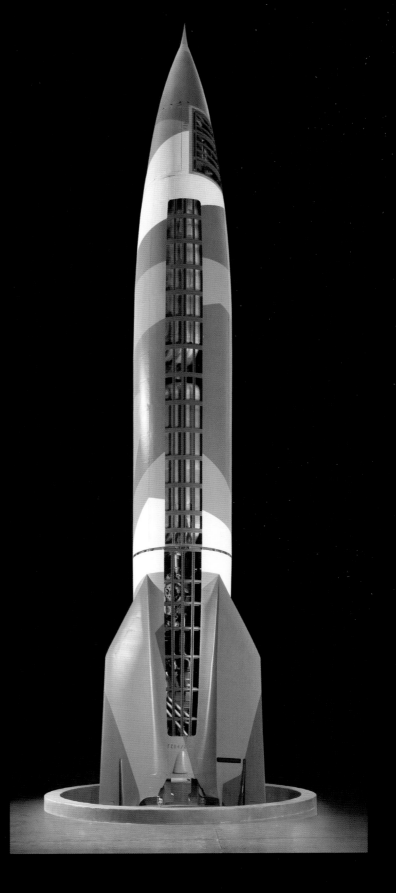

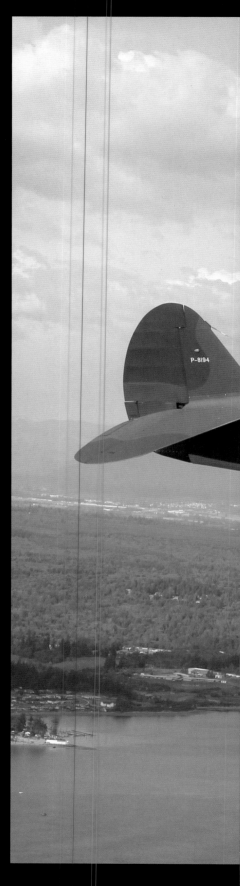

ABOVE: The winter months bustle with activity as each flying aircraft undergoes an extensive inspection. Though the vintage plane may have only logged a few more hours of flight time during the year, the FAA requires that FHC mechanics give every part of the plane get a thorough once-over.

RIGHT: The FHC's P-40 and Zero get ready to dive toward the crowd on a Fly Day. Though "Flying Tiger" pilots never encountered Zero aircraft in combat, they often mistakenly identified the Japanese combat planes they saw during dogfights as the famous naval fighter.

TOP: After each aircraft lands, mechanics go to work to complete post-flight maintenance and put the plane back on display in top condition. This often includes wiping a thin sheen of heated oil off the planes still-warm aluminum skin.

ABOVE: Parking the FHC's aircraft is a little like building a ship in a bottle. Each movement affects the planes parked around it. The FHC staff often has planning meetings to figure out which aircraft should be spotted where to accommodate test flights, maintenance, special events, and Fly Day performances.

continued from page 9

The FHC recruits pilots from all over the western United States. Most of them are ex-airline and/or military pilots who have dedicated thousands of flight hours to the operation of vintage warbirds. Some have flown in combat over Vietnam or Iraq, while others are former air race champions. At any one time, there are about ten expert pilots who fly for the FHC.

Paul Allen continues to collect and restore significant vintage aircraft. Commonly, each project is sent to a restoration company that is an expert in their field. For example, the Spitfire was restored in England while the Mustang was resurrected by one of the most highly skilled shops in the United States.

With an ever-expanding collection of exceptional artifacts and more on the way, the FHC ran out of space in the original hangar in 2012. A second hangar was built and opened one year later, in order to keep all finished and flyable aircraft in the public eye.

Exhibits in the original building cover the five World War II home fronts associated with the collection aircraft—Great Britain, United States, Russia, Japan, and Germany—focusing on the technological innovations and social situations seen in each country before and during the conflict. The exhibits in the second hangar tell the wartime stories of these planes. Fighting on five main fronts—western Europe, Eastern Front, Mediterranean, Pacific, and China-Burma-India—these aircraft technologies encountered some of the harshest fighting conditions and environments in the world.

The technology theme also allows the institution to examine more than just manned aircraft. Examples of Germany's pulse-jet-powered V-1 and a V-2 rocket allow visitors to see advanced tools of warfare in their earliest states. The V-1 is the world's first cruise missile, while the V-2 is the forerunner to the rockets that sent men to the moon. The parts used to rebuild these Nazi "vengeance weapons" were recovered from an underground production site in the Hartz Mountains of Germany.

Tanks and ground weapons, too, make up part of the growing collection. The Soviet T-34 and American M4A1 Sherman medium tanks illustrate some of the most successfully balanced blends of speed, size, weapons, and armor used by the Allies on the battlefield, while the compact *Hetzer* tank destroyer shows Germany's last-ditch efforts to stop them. Another iconic German weapon in the collection, feared by Allied tankers and pilots alike, is the Flak 37 88-millimeter gun. These cannon could blast shrapnel up to thirty thousand feet, or punch a hole through several inches of hardened tank armor.

Like the aircraft, the ground machines are all kept in working order. A highlight each spring is TankFest Northwest, where these weapons are driven and fired during a once-a-year public event.

The FHC cannot work without the assistance of volunteers. Nearly one hundred men and women take the time to assist the staff, running public events, giving tours of the facility, and acting as FHC ambassadors. Some of these volunteers are teenagers, while others were teens in the 1940s, and flew combat aircraft during World War II.

The FHC is open to the public every day from Memorial Day to Labor Day, and Tuesday through Sunday the rest of the year. The facility also includes a theater and gift shops stocked with a wide variety of books, models, and apparel. In the expansive working hangars, visitors of all ages can get up close to and personal with these rare treasures of the twentieth century while learning how the innovations of the past paved the way to today's modern aviation and aerospace technologies.

ABOVE: FHC warbird pilots Ross and "Bud" Granley pose for a photo on Father's Day, 2013. Both men flew with the Royal Canadian Air Force; Bud piloted F-86s and Ross flew CF-18s. After their military careers, both piloted passenger jets for United Airlines. Today, the father and son team operates the FHC's aircraft on Fly Days.

BELOW: Japan's pair of iconic fighters is posed for a photograph in front of the FHC's main hangar. The FHC is the only place in the world that a visitor can see these two famous aircraft together.

Though it took to the skies long after Britain's Spitfire and Germany's Messerschmitt Bf 109, US fighters like the Grumman F4F Wildcat were significantly behind the times. Only by leveraging its massive industrial might did America close the gap in

TECHNOLOGY OVER TIME

Visitors to the FHC encounter the following words when they enter the hangar lobby:

> Technology transforms society, but not at a constant rate. Occasionally, circumstances produce—demand—a sudden surge of innovation, yielding rapid and dramatic changes in society.
>
> One of those surges began during World War I and lasted through World War II, resulting in the planes you're about to see. Fully restored to flying condition, they represent advances in aviation and more broadly, in engineering, communications, manufacturing, and electronics—the building blocks of modernity.

In many ways, the changes brought about by the largest conflict in human history, World War II, have shaped our modern world. While historians agree that it was an era of rapid technological transformation, one has to look much farther into the past than the bombing of Pearl Harbor or the invasion of Poland to understand the advances in technology that took place during that war.

Even examining the period spanning the 1920s and 1930s won't reveal the entire picture. One could argue that World War II is the product of a long-ago age that most probably only learned about in school. Technologically speaking, it was the Industrial Revolution that put the world on a path toward the weapons and fighting styles seen in the 1940s.

TOP: A massive Beardmore V-12 engine is lowered into a Canada National Railways "oil-electric" locomotive in 1928. The sight would have been unthinkable to people living just a few generations before. In fact, even at the time, this huge machine regularly attracted large crowds of spectators along its route from Montreal to Toronto.

ABOVE: The old and new worlds collide. This image shows a "motorized smithy" in the St. Louis area in the 1930s. Though his trade centered around horses, he drove to jobs in the cab of his motorized truck, not a wagon.

As far back as the 1780s, many Western nations were moving from one milestone era to the next—from an existence based on manual labor and agriculture to a society and economy centered around production and machines.

While it might seem ridiculous to begin the story before Hitler or even his father were born, it is important to note that big changes often happen incrementally and have a delayed effect on history. Commonly, societies move slowly and cautiously, with each new development creating opportunities for further invention. Good ideas are often combined with contributions from many individuals over many decades.

Many ideas take years of "gestation time" to fully reach their potential. For example, a machine judged to be the first automobile was created around 1769. The first gasoline-burning engines were incorporated into auto designs around 1885. The first Model T, considered the first affordable and dependable motorcar, rolled from the Ford factory in 1908. And, even though the concept of an auto had been around for more than 130 years, there were still many more horses employed for transportation than there were cars in 1908.

While the Industrial Revolution may seem like far distant history to many of us, the second phase of the era is quite important toward understanding World War II. The era from 1871 to the outbreak of World War I (1914), dubbed the "Second Industrial Revolution," saw great advances in three technological areas—expanded transportation, wide-spread electrification, and refined production methods.

In the transportation field, one can see the rise of the first viable automobiles, a fully mature railroad system, great steamships, and, of course, the advent of the airplane. Though electricity seems less related to warfare, the availability of a dependable power source for tools, light, and movement helped change the face of production, which drastically affected the nature of clashes between nations.

World War I brought many of these Second Industrial Revolution developments to the forefront. Prior to that conflict, for example, each airplane was a sort of one-of-a-kind "work of art." That was not the case with World War I–era aircraft like the Curtiss Aeroplane & Motor Company's Jenny. One Jenny strut was built to fit exactly like another. These parts were mass-produced at a big factory—quickly and relatively easily.

In a time of world crisis, the gains made during the Second Industrial Revolution (transportation, electricity, and production) were coupled with great desire and urgency (world conflict). To continue to use Curtiss as an example, the company matured from making rickety Reims racers to pounding out literally thousands of "modern" trainer aircraft within five or six years. Similar examples can be seen in Europe, with Sopwith, Albatros, Fokker, and Nieuport all building tremendous numbers of aircraft.

However, most of the changes during World War I happened on the ground as the newly acquired strengths and techniques were coupled with a dire situation. Over a fairly brief period of time, the face of armed conflict changed as tanks, machine guns, deadlier artillery, poison gas, flame throwers, and viable submarines all became significant factors in warfare.

Military leaders were stunned. They were still fighting a nineteenth century-style war but were now encountering twentieth century equipment. The fight bogged down to a stalemate and both sides dug complex systems of trenches, protecting themselves from these new deadly weapons.

With a few exceptions, most of the fighting equipment employed in World War II had been used during World War I. Some, such as the flame thrower and machine gun, changed only a little, while others, like aircraft, made great leaps with twenty years of technological maturation. World War I

ABOVE: It is important to remember that the release of the Ford Model T was in no way the beginning of the automobile. Dozens of builders were making cars before Henry Ford perfected the production line. This relatively modern machine was cruising the streets of Paris in 1903.

BELOW: They are both steam engines, but things have improved with a century of development. This staged photo, taken in Chicago in 1933, shows a DeWitt Clinton locomotive from 1831 and Northern Pacific's newest behemoth, built 102 years later.

ABOVE: Workmen finish the job of installing a massive twenty-five-ton propeller on Cunard Line's newest ship; then simply called "hull number 534." When the ocean liner was launched later in 1934, she had been given the name RMS *Queen Mary*.

LEFT: American companies were not the only ones that harnessed the power of production for the Great War. In this image, French Nieuport fighters stretch to the horizon. When US pilots came overseas, they most often flew and fought in French- or British-built combat machines.

ABOVE: The Curtiss Aeroplane and Motor Company, circa 1917, was engaged in creating scores of aircraft using production-line methods. The Curtiss Jenny was considered America's first mass-produced aircraft. During World War I, Curtiss built not hundreds of airplanes, but thousands.

air fighting demonstrated most of the now familiar roles for combat aircraft (heavy bombers, attack aircraft, photo-reconnaissance, and fighters), though aircraft did not largely affect the outcome of that conflict. In the next war, things would be different. Aircraft would be involved in every major battle of World War II and were the deciding factor in many of them—the Nazi invasions in Europe, the Japanese bombing of Pearl Harbor, the American victory at Midway, and the United States' use of atomic bombs against Japan.

The interwar years became a perfect breeding ground for technological developments and improvements. Some of this was due simply to the legacy of past eras. The advances from the Second Industrial Revolution combined with impetus of "The Great War" made for a new age percolating with ideas and potential. Some new technologies were created, but in many cases, existing ideas were improved upon. Many of the milestone creations attributed to the interwar era were actually just significant pushes to make a known idea more useful, more viable, or available.

The automobile, invented years before, was coming into its own with a new infrastructure of roads and amenities, as well as improved assembly-line production methods spearheaded by the Ford Motor Company.

Flight, first demonstrated in 1903, really matured as Lindbergh crossed the Atlantic, aero-engines became more dependable, and the machines themselves were practical enough to transport people or cargo over long distances. By the mid-1930s, designers were making all-metal monoplanes very similar to the type that would be seen in World War II.

Radio, long attributed to the 1920s, was actually a known entity by the late nineteenth century. However, the 1920s was the era when 60 percent of American households purchased a radio for the first time, the first commercial broadcasts were made, and initial commercial radio stations were established.

While significant improvements stole the spotlight during the interwar era, it was also a period of invention, although many of these ideas made an impact later in the century during or after World War II.

The late 1920s saw the start of what would later become commercial television. In 1926, Robert H. Goddard launched the first modern, liquid-fuelled rocket. Enrico Fermi and his team achieved nuclear fusion experimentally in 1934. Rudimentary radar was installed on the ocean liner *Normandie* in 1935. In 1937, Frank Whittle ran his first jet engine. These were shades of things to come.

Militarily, the 1920s and 1930s were a period of continued development, especially in Europe. Many felt that the conflicts in Europe were not really resolved. Underlying tensions kept the innovations coming. Military leaders who fought in World War I worked to push, create, and keep their war machines current, believing that there would be more battles in the future. Even Germany, a country supposedly inhibited by World War I treaties, found ways to make new weapons. In many ways, this was similar to the climate seen *during* World War I—a time of technology and means, coupled with desire. But in this era, at least, the desire came from tensions and anticipation, not from all-out war.

The situation in the United States, however, was a bit different. Americans considered themselves separated from the ill-feelings among European nations. Even Japan's invasion of China on the other side of the Pacific Ocean seemed terribly

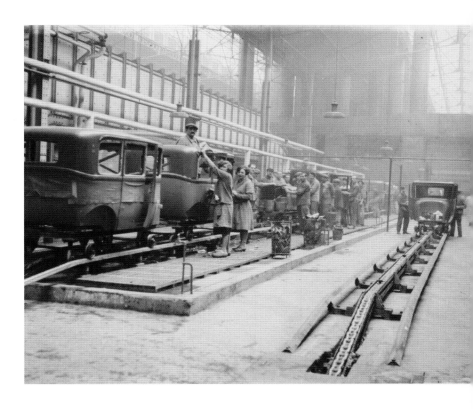

ABOVE: Soldiers with flame throwers, tanks, and deadly machine guns stopped antiquated infantry charges cold during World War I. In order to get away from these mechanized killing machines, opposing forces dug into the ground. Soldiers spent years in the trenches.

TOP RIGHT: By the 1920s, the concept of mass production was put into motion all over the world. This shot shows motorcars being assembled by men and women on a moving assembly line in Europe.

RIGHT: Radio had been around for decades, but it was popularized in the 1920s. This European unit works without an aerial or batteries. Plugged into household current, the user can "listen to broadcasts from London to Berlin."

ABOVE: The first Lockheed P-80 Shooting Star jet fighter flew in January 1944. Though some of the American jets were deployed to combat theaters by the end of World War II, none of the planes saw any fighting until the outbreak of the Korean War, five years later.

LEFT: In a burst of production before the fighting, nations like Great Britain put nearly all of the nation's resources into making the tools of war. Here, workers at the Bristol factory build Blenheim light bombers in the months before Germany attacked Poland.

remote. While agitators like "Billy" Mitchell warned of a nation falling behind, the people of America had had enough of war.

In the field of aviation, the contrast between nations on the potential front lines and those who were "isolationists" was startling. In 1935, Germany's Bf 109 and Britain's Hurricane flew for the first time. That same year, America's Grumman F3F Navy *biplane* fighter first took to the skies. America was behind by a full generation of aircraft development. In 1936, the Spitfire was introduced. More than a year and a half later, the Grumman F4F Wildcat and Brewster Buffalo flew for the first time in America. Those planes hardly deserve to be called "fighters" in the presence of a sleek machine such as the Spitfire.

When America finally entered World War II, the nation found that its fighters were inferior, its bombers couldn't protect themselves, its navy ships couldn't hunt German submarines effectively or win in a fair fight with their Japanese counterparts (especially at night), and its torpedoes were often nearly worthless. How did America make up the gap?

It was the very late 1930s and into the early 1940s before the United States began its true build-up for war, including producing equipment for France and Britain.

Luckily, the United States had the means, will, and resources to mobilize its great power and industry rather quickly. Their homeland was not under real threat of attack, as was the case for Russia, Britain, Germany, and Japan. The access to manpower, means of production, and relatively vast supplies of metals, gas, oil, and rubber made the United States a manufacturing powerhouse. In addition, America's ally, Britain, was a battle-seasoned nation—a veteran of real, "modern" fighting in Europe and the Middle East—able to help US leaders decide what needed to be done and how.

US projects often considered mid-war developments—the P-51 Mustang, F6F Hellcat, TBF Avenger, and B-29 Superfortress—all had their roots in this American burst of energy right before the start of conflict in Europe in 1939.

Again, we see a period of technological gestation. At the beginning of the shooting war for the United States, America had to fight with equipment it possessed before Pearl Harbor—F4F Wildcats, P-39 Airacobras, early model B-17s and B-25s, P-40 Tomahawks/Warhawks, etc. The late 1930s developments mentioned in the paragraph above came into the picture, roughly, around 1943. Results of the developments started

after Pearl Harbor—the P-80 Shooting Star, acceleration of the Manhattan Project, the first mass-produced helicopter (Sikorsky R-4)—appeared at the very end of the fighting.

Jet aircraft and helicopters, though extremely important to the military after World War II, had no real bearing on the outcome of that war. The atomic bomb, of course, was the exception.

Innovation during wartime isn't considered ideal and is typically frowned upon by many. Why? It takes money and resources away from proven equipment. A great example is the F6F. When it came time to make an up-rated version of the Hellcat naval fighter, the military told Grumman they could do it, and that the navy would be grateful, but please, please don't ever stop the assembly line. It was no time for radical (i.e. time-consuming) changes. The new F6F-5 exhibited very modest improvements over the F6F-3 as a result (strengthened tail, tighter cowling, new windscreen, water injection). The jump from P-51B to P-51D was equally as "low impact" on the factories.

The bulk of Japan's fighter force during World War II was made up of continuously upgraded versions of the Zero. Britain did the same with the Spitfire, and Germany with the Fw 190 and Bf 109. The latter changed the most. America had the luxury of trying many new projects on an accelerated basis: the P-40 gave way to the P-51, the F4F Wildcat was replaced

ABOVE: Production military helicopters, which would play an important role in Korea and Vietnam, had their roots in the innovations of World War II. Here, the Sikorsky XR-4 demonstrates shipboard landings on the SS *James Parker* in the summer of 1943. By the end of the war, some helicopters joined the fight with US forces abroad.

ABOVE: This striking photo shows a shipyard worker dwarfed by giant gears destined to be installed in American warships. The image was taken by the Office of War Information around 1943.

ABOVE: Slight evolutions in design, but not enough to stop production, can be seen in this flight of P-51 Mustangs over Europe. The oldest plane is the P-51B farthest from the camera. D-model P-51s had additional guns and an easily recognizable bubble canopy. With a cut-down fuselage, the fighters experienced more pronounced lateral stability issues. The newest Mustang in the photo, closest to the camera, has an added dorsal fin to quickly correct the problem without stopping the production line.

with the F6F Hellcat and F4U Corsair, and new *Essex* class fleet carriers took over for prewar carriers lost in the 1942 battles.

Some historians maintain that innovation during wartime can actually be harmful. Germany's leaders, desperate by the later stages of the war, were willing to entertain radical ideas (ideas that other nations would reject out of hand) hoping to change the course of the conflict. Some were quite successful. Conversely, though aircraft like jet planes were technologically advanced, German military leaders often asked, "What's better, fifteen more conventional Fw 190 fighters or a single new jet-powered Me 262?"

More peculiar projects, such as massive tanks and unconventional aircraft, consumed precious resources and manpower in Germany, often with little to show for it in the end. In some ways, the biggest winners in the World War II technology game were the Soviets and Americans, who swooped in to acquire Germany's data, innovations, and scientific minds after the war.

In the FHC aircraft, we see all stages of the development of combat planes before and during World War II. Quaint contraptions of fabric and cloth gave way to thundering all-metal war machines in just over a generation.

This amazing story of technological innovation has to open somewhere. We might as well start near the beginning.

The Curtiss JN-4D Jenny is the oldest plane at the FHC. The aircraft served both in military and civilian service in southern California. Wrecked many times over its long flying career, the Jenny was always valuable enough to be rebuilt to fly again.

THE BEGINNING

CURTISS JN-4D JENNY

POLIKARPOV U-2 (PO-2) LIGHT NIGHT BOMBER

All that it took was the threat of a world-sized war to free Glenn Curtiss from the Wright Brothers' lawyers. Since 1909, innovation in the field of aviation in the United States had been seriously hindered by the Wright Brothers' attempts to control the construction of flying machines. But with the nations of Europe on the verge of conflict, the US government became impatient with the petty fighting and patent litigation among aircraft builders. America needed warplanes and the government cleared the way for talented men like Curtiss to help.

The US military wanted tractor planes, aircraft with the engine and propeller up front. Curtiss had little experience with the type. His early planes were pushers, with the engine mounted behind the pilot. Unfortunately, when a pusher aircraft hit something, most often the ground, the hot engine and the immovable earth smashed together, often catching what the military considered the plane's most valuable item—a trained pilot—in between.

Curtiss turned to talent in England to help him with new aircraft. He hired a designer from Sopwith named B. Douglas Thomas, who designed the Curtiss Models J and N, both tractor aircraft. Still later, the best traits of each plane were combined into the model JN.

TOP: Pilots most often prefer to fly the Jenny from the back seat. The balance feels better and a flyer can see more of his surroundings too. Cutouts in the top and bottom wings allow the flyer to peek in directions that would be blocked from the front seat.

ABOVE: This image shows a row of Jenny aircraft equipped with gunner's rings in the aft cockpit. True to its training roots, the mounts appear to be equipped with cameras instead of guns in order to record student's skills at "shooting" from a moving plane.

The definitive version of the JN was the JN-4. The plane got its nickname from its coding, which looked a little like the name "Jenny." In the strictest sense, JNs were not combat planes. America's promise to "blacken the skies" over Germany with thousands of combat aircraft never came true. US combat flyers used French or English machines to "fight it out with the Hun over the trenches." However, those airmen needed to be trained, and some 95 percent of American and Canadian World War I combat pilots flew a Jenny when they learned to fly.

The Jenny's engine was not particularly powerful, so the plane was big. The machine needed every bit of the ninety horsepower produced by its OX-5 engine to pull two aviators (and occasionally machine guns, practice bombs, or a camera) into the skies. It was the opinion of some pilots that the JN-4D, with an upper wing spanning more than forty-three feet, was more of a motorized box kite than an aircraft.

To keep them light, aircraft of the day were covered in fabric. Though canvas was strong and readily available, airplane

ABOVE: The Jenny's rudder is blue, white, and red (front to back), similar to French World War I combat aircraft. British warplanes of the era had the same colors, but in the opposite order. To confuse the issue, stateside, Jenny trainers received rudders painted in both styles.

builders knew it was much too heavy to use as a covering. Silk, cotton, and linen—which weighed just three to six ounces per square yard—were popular choices.

The fabric was sealed for strength and durability, and to create a waterproof barrier to protect the airplane's interior structure. Early on, fabric coverings were sealed with a variety of substances, including rubber, linseed oil, banana oil, collodion, celluloid, and varnishes. Since many of the chemicals contained in these mixtures were quite toxic, airplane makers quickly began to call the sealers "dope," because breathing the fumes made them feel lightheaded, sick, or drunk.

Some areas on the aircraft were covered with other materials. Near the hot-running engine, fabric gave way to sheet metal. Any areas that were going to get extra wear were reinforced. The upper part of the cockpit and the "turtle back" area immediately behind it were sometimes strengthened with heavier fabric or a thin veneer of wood or metal to reinforce the places where the pilot climbed in and out.

The Jenny's underlying skeleton was primarily wood—ash, spruce, and birch were most common. The wooden components made up the ribs, spars, and stringers in the wings and longerons and frames in the fuselage. These were braced with thousands of feet of low tensile strength flexible steel wire (about 660 pounds of it). The complex web of wires gave the wooden structure nearly all of its strength and rigidity.

At the center of this mass of wood, wire, and fabric sat a pair of flyers; commonly a student up front and an instructor in the rear. Often, the novice pilot wore a helmet equipped with Gosport tubes, which ran from each ear hole to a funnel in the instructor's compartment, allowing the student to receive immediate and deafening orders. There was no way for a pupil to talk back, nor any need.

LEFT: The Jenny has handles on its bottom wing. Crewman used the handles to hold onto the big training airplane before the pilot was ready for takeoff. And, when the Jenny comes in for a landing, ground crews can catch the delicate aircraft by its wings and point it back toward the hangars.

BELOW: The Jenny has a wooden propeller sheathed in copper to protect it from damage. Operating from fields, a stray rock or dirt clod could initiate a crack or chip in the Jenny's prop that could grow into a real problem once the plane was in the air.

OPPOSITE: The wooden parts of the Jenny are made from hard and light wood varieties such as ash, spruce, and birch. When the plane lands in the grass, the plane's wooden skid (lined with a metal shoe) acts as a brake. Moving the Jenny into the FHC's concrete-floored hangar requires lifting the tail of the plane and placing the skid onto a small wheeled dolly.

During a Fly Day performance, the Curtiss JN-4 Jenny cruises over the crowd. Pilots say the antique plane is easy to fly but tricky to land. Unlike the heavier, faster aircraft, the aircraft is much more susceptible to sudden gusts of wind.

The Jenny's cockpit was a bit of a luxury. Early aircraft models left the pilot flying through the elements without protection and dangerously exposed in even the smallest of accidents. Flyers joked that, at least in a Jenny, you could hunker down below the rim of the cockpit and pretend you weren't about to crash.

This plane was also made to operate in the most primitive conditions. At the time, an airfield was truly a field. A flyer simply pointed his nose into the wind and "gave it the gun." The Jenny's wooden propeller was sheathed in copper to protect it from rocks and dirt clods as the plane roared to takeoff speed.

Landing on the grass was a bit dicier. Bamboo skids on the bottom wings protected the big plane should it start to go over, or ground loop. The plane had no brakes, so a metal shoe on the end of the wooden tailskid sliced through the grass, dirt, and mud, eventually stopping forward motion.

The Jenny was equipped with a simple bungee system to absorb some of the shock of landing. The plane's axle sat right above the lower union of its fore and aft landing gear struts. The stretchy chord holding the two parts together allowed the axle and wheels to bounce up and down. In fact, the axle would be caught and held in place by a metal bracket should the bungee snap during an extra-hard landing.

Hard landings were commonplace. Young flyers' inexperience, combined with a notoriously unreliable and underpowered engine, led to hundreds of Jenny "crack-ups." One of the only differences between the FHC's aircraft and a completely original World War I-era Jenny is the plane's engine. The collection's aircraft is fitted with an OXX6 power plant, a former blimp engine, which has a fraction more power, improved rocker arms, and a back-up ignition system for a bit of extra protection.

And, there were plenty of Jennys to crash. Curtiss Aeroplane Company of Hammondsport, New York, and six other firms, including a Canadian subsidiary, made 6,070 Jennys of all types. The plane is considered America's first truly mass-produced aircraft.

Sadly, just as the Wright versus Curtiss battles before World War I retarded the growth of America's aviation industry, the

WAS THE FHC'S JENNY A FAMOUS "BARNSTORMER?"

A detective would have a field day with one part of the story of the FHC's Jenny. The "never been cracked" aircraft fell into the hands of Earl Kampschmidt in 1925, and he kept the plane at Burdette Airport, the home of the famous 13 Black Cats, a company of flamboyant stunt pilots "who defied both superstition and the odds on survival" in the late 1920s. They often flew surplus Jenny aircraft in their wild barnstorming acts.

The Cats' menu of tricks was vast, including "parachute jumps, ship changes, upside down flying, delayed opening jumps, ocean landings, rope ladder, and wing walking." For many of their eye-popping, and often illegal stunts, the 13 Black Cats preferred to use battered Jennys, which they could beg or borrow from members, friends, and colleagues.

There is no direct evidence that Kampschmidt had anything to do with these hell-raisers, but soon after he arrived at Burdette, his plane encountered a string of bad luck. He wrote the Department of Commerce, "The propeller, landing gear, and left lower [wing] were replaced after a stall close to the ground." Then after he had rebuilt the plane from that accident, he described another incident: "A strong wind, one night, turned the ship over on its back, breaking the front beam in the left upper wing near the tip."

Luckily no one was hurt in these many accidents. As Cats member Reginald Denny wrote, "Defying superstition, daring fate, that's what it was. A black cat has ever been regarded as the harbinger of disaster."

As one of the boys gives the propeller a whirl, everyone else hangs on. With no brakes, it was important to keep the Jenny under control until the pilot is ready to go.

availability of "still new-in-the-box" Jennys made postwar innovation slow going in the United States. Why buy a new airplane when you could get an existing Jenny for as little as fifty dollars?

After military service, many of the trainer planes found a new career in barnstorming. Ex-army aviators traveled the country, introducing the masses to aviation. Secondhand, often modified, Jennys became synonymous with the swash-buckling aviators of the "air circus" who sold rides and participated in risky, outlandish stunts.

The FHC's Curtiss JN-4D Jenny, serial 3712, flew in both worlds—military and civilian. It was one of 252 JN planes built at Curtiss in May 1918. Each plane, without engine, cost the government an average of $3,155.24.

PREVIOUS PAGES: The Jenny's OX-5-type engine was not what you'd call overly powerful or particularly dependable. It requires constant attention before and after flights, and Curtiss recommended that it be overhauled often. Luckily, the FHC's aircraft only takes short hops during the summer and is treated with kid gloves. INSET: The rear cockpit of the Curtiss Jenny carries a full but basic complement of flight instruments including a clock, altimeter, oil pressure gauge, RPM, water temperature, and a compass. The control stick looks very similar to the handle of a vintage baseball bat.

BELOW: The Jenny's tail skid is fine in the grass, but airports are paved these days. Mechanics have created a special cradle to bring the World War I-era plane back home to the FHC's hangar.

The plane was crated and delivered to March Field near Riverside, California, by June 1918 where it was used to train army flyers. Second Lieutenant Topliff Olin Paine learned to fly at March Field while the FHC's Jenny was there. Today, the Jenny resides at Paine Field, named after the late military and airmail pilot.

In late 1918, March Field had ninety-nine Jenny training aircraft in service with more in reserve. The FHC's Jenny was rated "good" in the spring of 1919 by army inspectors and had logged "253:48 hours" of operating time. It was sold back to Curtiss on May 6, 1919, in order to be refurbished for civilian sale.

By 1925, the plane was back in Southern California. Licensing paperwork reveals that the plane, which had "never been cracked" according to the owner, was purchased by Earl Kampschmidt, who wrecked it twice soon after.

The plane stayed a wreck until 1937. Undaunted by the letter from the Department of Commerce warning him that the Jenny was old, had terrible spin characteristics, and should be thoroughly inspected, Ross Hadley enlisted a mechanic and a class at a junior college to put the plane back in the air. He was flying by late 1939.

By 1940, the Jenny was on its third engine and was prohibited from "intentional aerobatics," according to an inspection report. The airworthiness certificate expired in October 1941. When the CAA requested information on the aircraft in 1947, they were notified that the airplane had been destroyed in a hangar fire at Van Nuys Airport in October 1943.

However, like the phoenix, the Jenny would rise again. What remained of the aircraft was sold (for one dollar) to Sammy Mason of the Hollywood Hawks. He wrote that the plane would "be used for movie and airshow purposes for wing walking and aerobatics. It will be flown cross country to and from airshows but will not be flown over populated areas."

After two more accidents, in 1947 and 1948, the plane ended up in the hands of a scrap dealer in Rosemead, California. Jack Hardwick made his living selling parts from World War II surplus military planes. Dismantled, what was left of the Jenny remained in storage until the mid-1970s.

Ray Folsom had always wanted a Jenny. His father had flown in World War I and had owned a surplus JN-4D when Ray was a young boy. Folsom rented other aircraft he owned to movie and TV companies, including a Standard J-1 trainer that appeared in the movie *The Great Waldo Pepper*.

Folsom did not find his Jenny until an acquaintance purchased a large collection of antique aircraft and parts, which included what became the FHC's aircraft. The plane was "essentially intact, which was unusual for so old a machine." Folsom spent about five years restoring the airplane and then put it to work in Hollywood.

In early 1999, the FHC purchased the nearly complete Jenny from Folsom. The plane was moved to Vintage Aviation Services in Kingsbury, Texas for restoration in accordance to the collection's strict standards.

Beyond a general overhaul, some damaged structural areas were rebuilt and items that were determined inauthentic were restored. Flight testing on the rebuilt Jenny began in late 2001. The plane was eventually shipped to Washington and is currently on display at the collection's facility in Everett. The plane takes to the air regularly during Fly Days in the summer, flying off the grass at Paine Field.

The Jenny never went to war, but another aircraft that began its life as a training plane saw plenty of action during World War II and beyond. On the other side of the globe, the Soviet government tasked aircraft designer Nikolai Nikolaevich Polikarpov with creating a replacement for the U-1, a rudimentary two-seat trainer.

His 1927 prototype, designated the U-2, was too simple, too weighty, and could barely get off the ground.

An improved version built the following year retained some of the best features of the original. Those at the airfield, watching the little plane putter into the skies, would have been astonished to know that there was going to be thirty-three thousand more built over three decades.

BELOW: Sunlight passes through the Jenny's skin, revealing the wood structure underneath. One of the lightest planes in the FHC collection, the Jenny weighs about 1,920 pounds loaded. By comparison, a standard Honda automobile weighs 1,000 pounds more.

ABOVE: In a moment of downtime, female Soviet combat flyers discuss the night's actions while one of their trusty Po-2 bombers awaits another mission over enemy lines.

LEFT: The FHC's Po-2 is equipped with Venturi tubes on either side of the cockpit. As air passes through the funnel-shaped constriction, its velocity increases while pressure decreases. The suction system was a cheap and simple way to power the plane's vacuum-driven gyroscope.

ABOVE: The Po-2 was often equipped with six small bomb racks to carry light bombs. Often, the plane's gunner carried more explosives in her lap, tossing them out as the plane conducted its diving bomb run on enemy troops.

In many ways, the U-2 was quite similar to the Jenny from ten years before; a two-place biplane with fixed gear. However, the Russian-built version incorporated various improvements.

The radial engine was slightly more powerful and much more dependable than the OX-5. It allowed the airframe to be more compact than the "box kite" Curtiss aircraft. The U-2 wings were a bit more complex and compressed, but their construction was similar to that of the Jenny—a wooden skeleton covered in fabric. The majority of the fuselage on the U-2 was skinned with metal or plywood, making the plane more durable and allowing the structure to carry less load. Some portions of the aircraft used metal entirely, including the undercarriage and several bracing components.

Outwardly, the U-2 was similar to many inexpensive and simple aircraft of the time—fixed gear, tail skid, open cockpits, and wooden propeller. Russia's military and civilian organizations adopted the U-2 to teach young flyers the basics of aviation.

As with many successful aircraft, it didn't take long to dream up a multitude of new uses for the U-2. The little plane's resume soon expanded to include crop duster, ambulance, scout aircraft, liaison plane, patrol machine, passenger plane, and photography platform. In the wilds of Russia, flyers often affixed floats or skis in the place of its tires.

The military, too, figured that the plane could do more than train pilots. A machine gun synched to fire through the propeller arc was added on the left side of the fuselage.

ABOVE: The Po-2's simple five-cylinder engine roars to life at the beginning of a Fly Day performance at the FHC. The plane's Shvetsov engine has a distinct buzz, which American servicemen likened to the sound of a sewing machine.

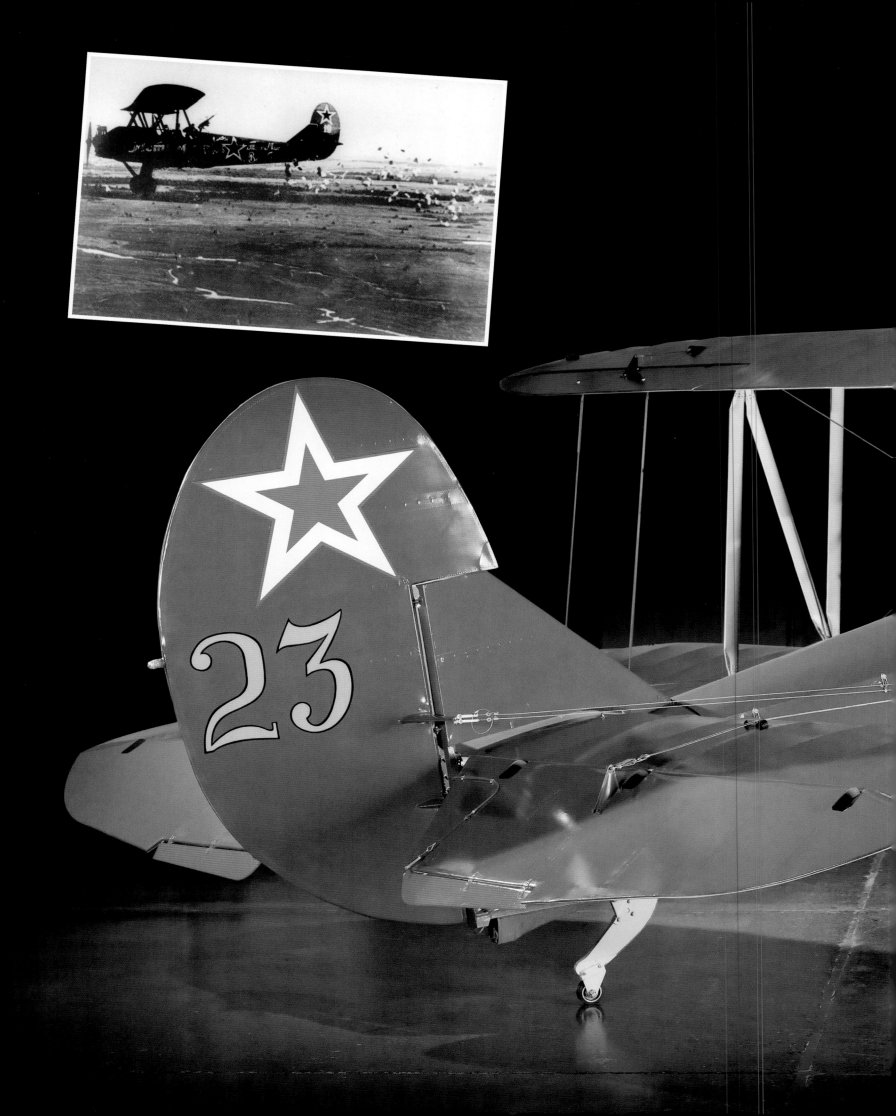

PREVIOUS PAGES: The FHC's Po-2 can be equipped with a tail wheel or a tail skid, allowing the plane to be flown from Paine Field's nine-thousand-foot paved runway or from a simple grass field. INSET: Like many successful combat aircraft, the Polikarpov was drafted into completing a multitude of aerial tasks. Here, a Po-2's flight crew drops propaganda leaflets over the front lines.

Two-hundred-kilogram bomb racks were fitted under the wings, and a 7.62mm machine gun cropped up near the back seat for protection.

Of course, when Hitler's Germany invaded Russia in 1941, both civilian and military U-2s were enlisted to help the massive war effort. Fragile and vulnerable to gunfire, U-2s were also ridiculously slow, which actually allowed a skilled pilot to avoid becoming prey to a fast-flying Messerschmitt fighter. Hard turns and ground-hugging swerves at well below the speedy attacker's stall speed gave a German flyer only a split second to line up a clean shot.

Tricks aside, the U-2 was most useful in the dark. The plane is perhaps most famous as an LNB—light night bomber. Many U-2 units were "manned" almost entirely by female combat pilots. Inflicting around-the-clock harassment and psychological warfare was at the heart of this endeavor. U-2 flyers would cruise over enemy lines, searching for German activity below. In the cold Russian wilderness, small fires often gave invaders away.

The pilot would cut the engine to idle and glide. The U-2 could coast "downhill" as steady as a rock, a useful trait from its training days. At the right moment, the pilot would spring the bombs free from their racks. Her companion, in the back cockpit, might toss out a few small bombs or grenades herself. Then, as the spotlights came on and the anti-aircraft shells started flying, the U-2 pilot would gun her engine and make a quick escape.

The German soldiers, up all night to the sounds of gunfire, bombs, and the putter of that sewing machine five-cylinder engine, called the intruders *Nächthexen*—"Night Witches."

The flyers had a wicked job. The U-2 was agonizingly slow, painfully delicate, and horrifically flammable. Putting all those

ABOVE LEFT: The FHC's pair of Polikarpov-designed aircraft fly in formation in this rare photo. Though built for completely different tasks, both aircraft saw extensive service with the Soviet Air Forces during combat on the Eastern Front.

LEFT: At a landing speed of about 67 kilometres per hour (42 mph), the Po-2 prepares to touch down on Paine Field's runway 34L during a photo session.

OPPOSITE: The Po-2's dual cockpit allowed for two flyers—a pilot in front and a gunner behind. The crew climbed into the aircraft using the reinforced wooden walkway built over the plane's delicate fabric-covered wing.

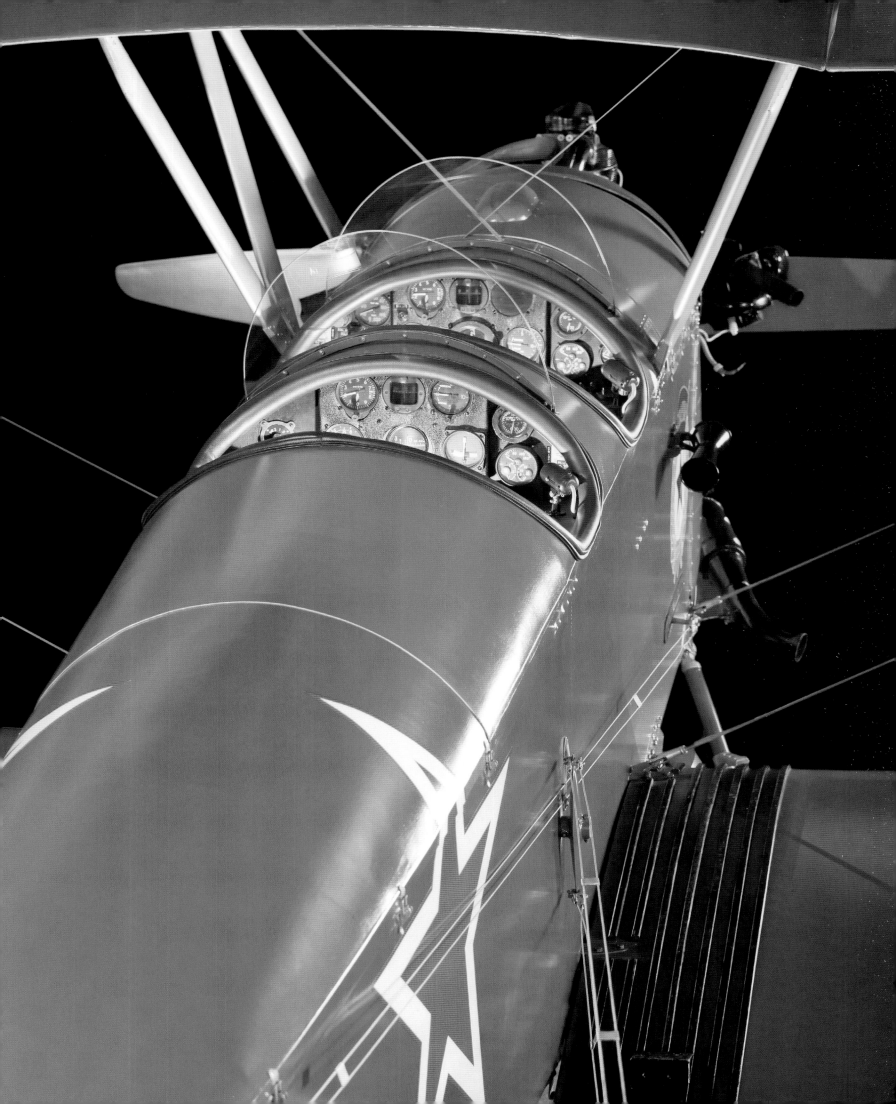

terrifying traits aside, the pilot and gunner in a U-2 were also, nearly always, unfathomably cold. Russia, while geographically diverse, isn't exactly known for its balmy evenings. Flying the U-2 was like driving in a convertible at eighty miles an hour in a snowstorm. And the plane could not carry much weight, so these women braved the enemy and the cold as many as eight or nine times a night.

When designer Nikolai Nikolaevich Polikarpov died in July 1944, the U-2 was redesignated to honor him. The scrappy little plane became known as the Polikarpov Po-2.

The FHC's Po-2 was built in Russia that same year. Little is known about the history of this aircraft during World War II. Presumably it was used by the Soviet Air Force on the Eastern Front, then abandoned after being damaged beyond economical repair in an accident or in combat.

The aircraft was located in the area of Belarus in the Soviet Union, east of Poland, which became a sovereign nation in 1990. The wreck was retrieved and restored by members of the Polish Aero Club, a large association of sportsmen and recreational flyers based in Warsaw, in 1995.

A warbird specialist familiar with Po-2 aircraft will note the use of some materials in the restored aircraft are most often seen in Polish versions of the Po-2 (designated CSS-13s), including metal struts in place of the original tube and wood braces. As well, an up-rated Polish version of the M-11 engine, produced in 1954, has been substituted for the World War II-era Shvetsov motor. M-11 engines, as well as Po-2 type aircraft, were made under license in Poland for many years.

The FHC acquired the Po-2 in 2000. Today, the plane is painted to represent loosely the scheme of a 46th Guards Bomber Regiment aircraft. The 46th was the only all-woman Red Army regiment during World War II and had a total cadre of over two hundred. The roughly thirty aircrews flew over twenty-four thousand combat missions over 1,100 nights during the war.

The plane's paint scheme includes the number "23" on the tail. Some thirty women flyers in the Soviet Air Force earned

ABOVE: A Soviet flyer hand-props the Po-2's engine at the start of a long, cold bombing mission against German invaders during combat on the Eastern Front.

LEFT: The front cockpit of the FHC's World War II-era Po-2 has a mount for a modern hand-held radio affixed near the right hand of the pilot.

the Hero of the Soviet Union medal by the end of World War II, "the highest distinction in the Soviet Union awarded personally or collectively for heroic feats in service to the Soviet state and society." Of these thirty, twenty-three of them were Night Witches of the famous 46th Guards Bomber Regiment, with five awarded posthumously. A twenty-fourth woman flyer was awarded the medal posthumously in 1995.

The words painted in Russian Cyrillic letters on the port side of the Po-2 can be translated roughly as "Revenge for Dusya," a reference to Dusya Nosal, a Russian female aviator considered the "best pilot" in the 46th by her fellow flyers. She was killed in combat while flying a Po-2 when a Focke-Wulf fighter pounced on her aircraft.

The legacy of the Po-2 lasted far beyond World War II. Thousands of the planes were built through 1952 in the Soviet Union, and even longer in Poland. United Nations servicemen in Korea found that the Night Witch routine worked as well in the 1950s as it had during the earlier conflict. North Korean Po-2s, supplied by the Soviet Union, often buzzed American bases at night during the Korean War, and became known as "Bed Check Charlies" by the servicemen.

ABOVE: Over Puget Sound, FHC pilot "Bud" Granley slides the Polikarpov Po-2 into formation for a quick photograph during a test flight.

Solving the issue of a small, slow intruder was perhaps even harder for the Americans with their high-tech weapons than it was for the Germans. Radar-equipped fighters often scrambled to chase these shadows in the night but more often than not, they came home empty-handed. The bombings continued, and the last American military men killed overseas in an enemy aerial attack were bombed by a Bed Check Charlie at the base on the island of Cho-do, off the Korean coast, on April 15, 1953.

RIGHT: The exhaust valves in the bottom cylinders of the Po-2's radial engine are known to seep oil. Here, mechanics use stove pipes over the lower exhaust stacks to guide the oily smoke away from the plane's fuselage at startup.

The Polikarpov I-16 fighter was a mixture of cutting-edge design and conventional traits of the era. Observers joked that the fighter was simply a huge engine with parts of an airplane following behind in close formation.

THE PRIMITIVES

2

POLIKARPOV I-16 TYPE 24 *RATA*

HAWKER HURRICANE MK.XII

Given enough power, even a barrel will fly. The Polikarpov I-16 Type 24 *Rata* certainly fit this description. This pudgy little machine was very modern for its time, but still retained more than a few antiquated traits.

Why such a leap in design? It is fair to say that Nikolai Polikarpov was highly motivated by outside forces. Soon after creating the Po-2 and various biplane fighters in the late 1920s, Joseph Stalin, the all-powerful leader of the Soviet Union, decided Polikarpov and his engineering team were not meeting expectations. As a result, Polikarpov was arrested and sentenced to death on trumped-up charges of sabotage and counter-revolutionary activities. Later, the sentence was reduced to ten years of hard labor. He began working on the radically new I-16 fighter during his time in prison.

This plane was a bulbous brute dominated by a massive radial engine. The first version of the machine was powered by a Russian copy of a Bristol Jupiter nine-cylinder powerplant. As with the Gee Bee racing planes of the era, a flyer really had to struggle to see around the nose while taxiing.

The I-16, coming at the end of the biplane era, was the first of the next chapter in fighter design—a cantilevered monoplane with retractable landing gear. "Cantilevered" meant all of the wing's structure was inside the skin, so that speed-robbing struts, wires, and supports howling in the slipstream no longer caused drag.

In oversimplified terms, the I-16 was much like the Polikarpov I-15 biplane fighter, but without the top wing. Losing the upper wing, struts, and wires gave the monoplane a more than one-hundred-miles-per-hour speed advantage over its older brother.

The plane's fully retractable landing gear factored into that speed equation too. A cable led from each wheel to a crank at the pilot's right hip. It took forty-four muscle-busting turns to draw the wheels up into the wings. On takeoff, I-16s would often wobble, pitching slightly up and down, as a flyer worked the landing gear crank.

The I-16 was a mix of materials similar to the Po-2 from five years earlier. The fuselage was primarily wood, with a birch strip skin bonded with glue called *shpon*. The skin was 4mm thick near the nose and tapered to just 2.5mm at the tail. The wings were made of metal and mainly fabric-covered.

BELOW: In an effort to make the I-16 as speedy as possible, the fighter's Shvetsov engine and prop hub are almost completely covered by a metal shroud. In the center of the spinner is a Hucks starter—used by ground crew to mechanically start the engine.

The plane had cartoonishly big wings and tail. Control surfaces, not far from the fighter's center of gravity, needed to be large to work effectively. However, Polikarpov didn't go too far; the skittish I-16 was known to be highly maneuverable because it was naturally unstable.

The first I-16s had an enclosed cockpit but biplane era pilots hated being closed in; they felt separated from the seat-of-the-pants flying they were used to. When the I-16's canopy started to fog over, it was the final straw. Designers reverted back to an open cockpit configuration to meet pilot demands.

Drop-down doors on either side of the cockpit allowed a pilot to lean out to see around the massive nose both on the ground and even in the air. Soviet manuals stated, "Do not be shy or embarrassed to open the side doors in flight prior to landing to help you see out."

Despite his cruel treatment by Soviet leaders, Polikarpov had created another astounding success. The I-16 became

ABOVE: With such cold conditions in western Russia, it is only natural that some I-16 fighters would be converted to fly with skis. On this version, a Type 5, the skis were fixed, but later *Rata* aircraft flew with a set of retractable skis.

LEFT: Restoration and maintenance chief Jason Muszala coaxes the I-16's engine to life outside the FHC's hangar door during an engine test. Oil collected in the cylinders of a radial engine often makes for puffs of blue smoke when the plane is first fired up.

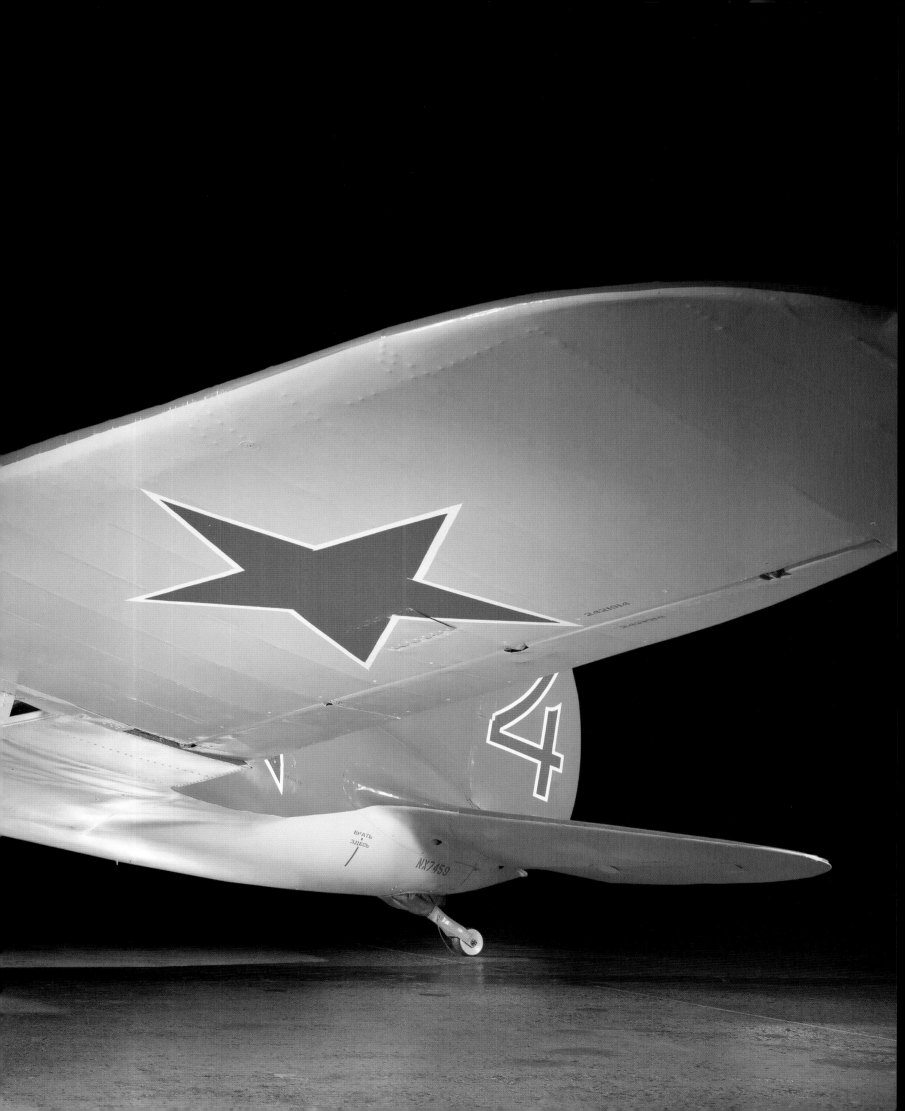

ABOVE: FHC pilot Carter Teeters takes the Polikarpov I-16 on a test flight near Paine Field. Built with small control surfaces, the *Rata* is naturally unstable and requires constant attention while it is in the air.

PREVIOUS PAGES: The I-16 had fabric-covered wings and a plywood fuselage. Yet the pint-sized fighter is incredibly weighty and solid. During combat, Soviet pilots would sometimes ram enemy aircraft with their hearty *Ratas*.

the Soviet Army's main fighter type from 1934 to 1941—and, the Red Air Force was busy during this period. Even before the German invasion of the Soviet Union, I-16s flew in the Spanish Civil War, the Russo-Japanese and Sino-Japanese conflicts in the late 1930s, and the Winter War with Finland. Everywhere it went, it seemed, the odd little plane gathered another nickname.

The men who flew it in Spain called it *mosca* (fly), while those who fought against it knew it as *rata* (rat). The Japanese called it *abu* (gadfly) and the Germans *dienstjäger* (duty fighter). Russians called it *yastrebok* (young eagle) or *ishak* (little donkey).

Though obsolete by the time World War II began, the little plane soldiered on, fighting against more sophisticated German aircraft on the Eastern Front. Soviet pilots resorted to ramming German bombers with their solid I-16s when outnumbered and out of ammunition. The least dangerous method involved a Soviet pilot striking an enemy plane with part of his own, bumping it with his wing for example. Other pilots chose to use their propeller to chop into the control surfaces of a fleeing German bomber. The most dangerous method was the "direct attack"—an all-out collision with an enemy plane. If a pilot was skilled, and very lucky, he might survive the intentional crash and bail out.

The FHC's I-16, a Type 24, is a late version of the fighter. It had a tail wheel instead of the earlier tailskid, an improved engine, and could carry rockets and external fuel tanks. Most I-16s, including the collection's aircraft, were built at Plant

No. 21 in Nizhny Novgorod. This aircraft came off the assembly line in July 1940 and most likely went right into combat in northwest Russia.

The full story of the loss of the FHC I-16 may never be known but it is interesting to note that the location of the wreck corresponds with a dogfight that took place overhead on August 13, 1941, between Soviet and Finnish pilots. In the melee, two I-16s were lost.

Historians following the career of Flt. Mstr. Yrjö Turkka, a Finnish ace of the 24 Squadron, wrote about the scramble to intercept Soviet bombers with a group of five BWs (Finnish Brewster Buffaloes) near the Finnish front line.

"At Soanlahti the Finnish pilots spotted five twin-engine bombers flying in opposite course, a little higher. Lt. Sarvanto ordered everyone to climb and stand by for attack. When the BWs were 300m above the bombers they were also 200m behind, 'Zamba' [Turkka] rocked his wings as the signal to attack: the BWs dived . . ."

"During the dive, the Finnish pilots spotted a trio of I-16 fighters heading in to break up their attack. The BW pilots split up, some staying on the bombers and others taking on the I-16s. After a drawn-out dogfight, Turkka managed to destroy one of the I-16s."

"The burst of the focused 0.5" [.50-caliber] machine guns hit the fuselage of the I-16 between the cockpit and the engine, and the Soviet fighter caught fire. Turkka decreased power and flew on the wing of the I-16, so close that he could see the face of the enemy pilot who kept flying in level flight. The Soviet pilot turned his head and looked at the Finnish pilot, then the flames burst in the cockpit and at the face of the pilot. He lifted one hand to protect his face, then turned his fighter upside down and dived into the terrain. The fuel tank of the I-16 exploded in a fireball that ignited the surrounding forest.

"All five fighters came and continued for Joensuu. In debriefing it was found that two DB-3s had been shot down, as well as two I-16s, the other one by Sgt. Kinnunen."

The wreck of the FHC aircraft was found just a few miles away from Turkka's combat, near the northwest shore of Lake Yaglyayarvi.

Sir Tim Wallis—a New Zealand flyer and entrepreneur, who established the New Zealand Fighter Pilots Museum, the popular Wings Over Wanaka air show, and the Alpine Deer Group (including the Alpine Fighter Collection)—was investigating warbird wrecks shortly after the breakup of the Soviet Union in the 1990s. He conceived the idea of recovering and restoring Soviet aircraft while others were focused on Allied Lend-Lease aircraft found in Russia. Six I-16s were recovered and restored in the early to mid-1990s by Avio Restorations and the Aeronautical Research Bureau and Plant in Novosibirsk. The latter is located at Plant No. 153, which produced some

ABOVE: These clean, almost-too-pristine I-16 aircraft were photographed in flight for a 1941 Soviet propaganda film with the pithy title, *The Soviet Red Army Air Force Guards the Frontiers of the Motherland.*

FOLLOWING PAGES: It was always very difficult to see around the I-16's massive engine. Drop-down doors allowed a pilot to lean to each side—even while flying. INSET: The spartan cockpit of the I-16 featured a padded leather sill, a two-hand control stick, and, off to the right, a manual crank for the fighter's retractable landing gear.

ABOVE: From this shot, it is easy to see why some flyers called the Hurricane the "hunchback." The fighter's slightly bent appearance put the pilot at the top of the fuselage, giving a good view of the world around him from the cockpit.

I-16s during the war. Interestingly, two of the men involved in the restoration project had been fifteen-year-old workers at the factory in 1941 when the I-16s were still being produced.

The collection's I-16 was the fifth I-16 to be restored. Each plane was flight-tested and certified in Russia before being disassembled and exported to New Zealand. There, the planes were reassembled and flight-tested. The FHC I-16 was registered as ZK-JIQ on October 9, 1997 and flew with four other I-16s at the Warbirds over Wanaka air show in 1998.

A photo of the collection's future I-16 was featured in a full-page ad in *Warbirds Journal* in July 1998. The Alpine Fighter Collection ad states, "[T]his is one of THE significant fighters to re-appear from oblivion." The plane was acquired by the FHC as part of a four-aircraft deal with the Alpine Deer Group of New Zealand in August 1998.

The I-16 remains one of the most exotic and unusual aircraft seen in the FHC. More familiar but no less interesting is the Hawker Hurricane, which many Americans saw flying regularly in the pages of *Life* magazine even before the United States entered World War II.

Airmen joked that the Hurricane was so old that it started life as a biplane. It was actually the other way around. The Hurricane was a monoplane version of the double-decker Hawker Fury fighter just like the I-16 was a monoplane offshoot of the Polikarpov I-15 biplane.

Hawker Aircraft Limited chief designer Sydney Camm took on the project of modernizing the Fury as a private venture in 1933, even before the Royal Air Force (RAF) had formally asked for it. The single-winged Fury, renamed Hurricane, became

RIGHT: The "fin flash" on the Hurricane is a throwback to World War I, when the entire rudders of many Allied planes were covered with bold vertical stripes. The recognizable stripes were supposed to keep British pilots from accidently bouncing French aircraft (or vice versa) in cases of mistaken identity. Many planes continued to carry a small block of colors, more as tradition than identification, up through World War II and beyond.

PREVIOUS PAGES: The FHC's Hawker Hurricane Mk XII is a rare example built in Canada. Made to be launched from a ship on a one-way mission, the fighter was never called upon to sacrifice itself in order to save an Allied merchant ship convoy. INSET: In the starboard wing of this "Hurri-bomber," just inboard of the guns, is the housing for the plane's G.45 gun camera. The small twelve-volt recorder saw action in Hurricanes and many other British fighters of the era.

BELOW: In this image, the Hurricane reveals its biplane heritage. Nearly all the surfaces behind the pilot are skinned in fabric. Also note the fixed tail wheel—permanently hanging below the fighter.

the first monoplane fighter used by the RAF and the first RAF fighter to fly at over three hundred miles per hour.

The plane had many of the construction traits of the planes of the late 1920s and early 1930s. Like the I-16, the aircraft was a mixture of wood, steel, and fabric. The core of the new fighter was a high-tensile steel tube frame that was mechanically assembled without welds. Unlike the monocoque skins of many modern fighters, in which the stressed metal skin carries much of the structural load, the inner structure of the

Hurricane was similar to the composition and appearance of a railroad bridge. A wooden framework covered that stout skeleton with metal skin near the nose and fabric from the trailing edge of the wings aft.

Some Allied pilots, particularly those flying sleek-looking Spitfires, called Hurricanes "hunchbacks" because of their bowed appearance while sitting on the ground. In flight, the odd shape was an advantage because the pilot sat high—giving him a good view from the cockpit.

The wings of the Hurricane prototype were steel structures covered in fabric. However, later versions of the aircraft used stressed metal skins for better performance. The Hurricane's designers mounted the plane's glycol and oil coolers in the big scoop under the fighter's belly.

A highlight of the new fighter was the Rolls-Royce Merlin engine. The Hurricane and Spitfire, of Battle of Britain fame, used the dependable and powerful V-12.

Other traits of the new Hurricane included a wide-track

SUICIDE SORTIE

The Flying Heritage Collection's Hawker fighter plane began its life as a Sea Hurricane: an aircraft made to be launched from a ship as last-ditch protection against a marauding enemy patrol bomber. Out at sea, merchant ships were hundreds of miles from any land-based aircraft protection. German long-range Focke-Wulf Condor bombers could intercept Allied convoys outside the range of fighter cover and wreak havoc. In the last part of 1940, these attacks sunk over a half million tons of Allied shipping.

ABOVE: A "Hurricat" fighter launches into the skies with the help of rocket power during testing. These catapults were later mounted on the decks of ships to protect ship convoys from German patrol aircraft.

The solution was for convoys to bring their own cover. The Royal Navy invented the Catapult Aircraft Merchantmen (CAM) ship in the period before the advent of the escort carrier. "Hurricats," as the sea-going planes were sometimes called, were perched on a trolley riding on a bow-mounted catapult rail. The trolley was propelled by thirteen rockets fired by the Catapult Directing Officer after the pilot dropped his arm to signal readiness. Some thirty-five CAM ships operated between May 1941 and July 1943.

A Hurricane fighter, hurtled into the skies from a ship, was more than a match for the slower and bigger Condor bombers. Sometimes, even the sight of a rocket-powered launch was enough for German attack aircraft to move away in search of easier targets.

Victory, however, was only half the battle. After a fight, a Sea Hurricane pilot had to make some very hard choices. He could set a course for the nearest land, or if the ships were too far out at sea, he had to ditch his plane or jump. Bailing out was dangerous, but the frozen waters of the North Atlantic were even worse. A pilot had to pick just the right moment to leave the plane, because he wasn't going to last long in the water.

Flyers were originally drawn from volunteers in the Fleet Air Arm, but, after the Battle of Britain, many of the pilots on the CAM ships were RAF combat veterans.

The CAM ship concept worked. Hurricane pilots officially shot down six Condors and damaged many others. Still more enemy attackers were driven away by the new convoy protection. The cost was high. Many flyers and aircraft were lost while attempting to keep the sailors and their supply ships safe.

The collection's Sea Hurricane, of course, was never launched into the cold skies over the North Atlantic. Eventually, the plane went back to the aircraft factory for reconditioning and it started the next stage of its career.

ABOVE: Early-model Hurricanes are lined up for inspection in France, circa 1939. Some of the first batches of Mk.I Hurricanes had Venturi tubes on their sides and wooden, two-bladed, fixed-pitch Watts propellers.

RIGHT: Mechanics say that working on the Hawker Hurricane is a challenge. A multitude of the plane's systems are stuffed into the voids between the plane's engine and steel tube structural members. This image was taken as the FHC's Hurricane was being prepped for a test flight.

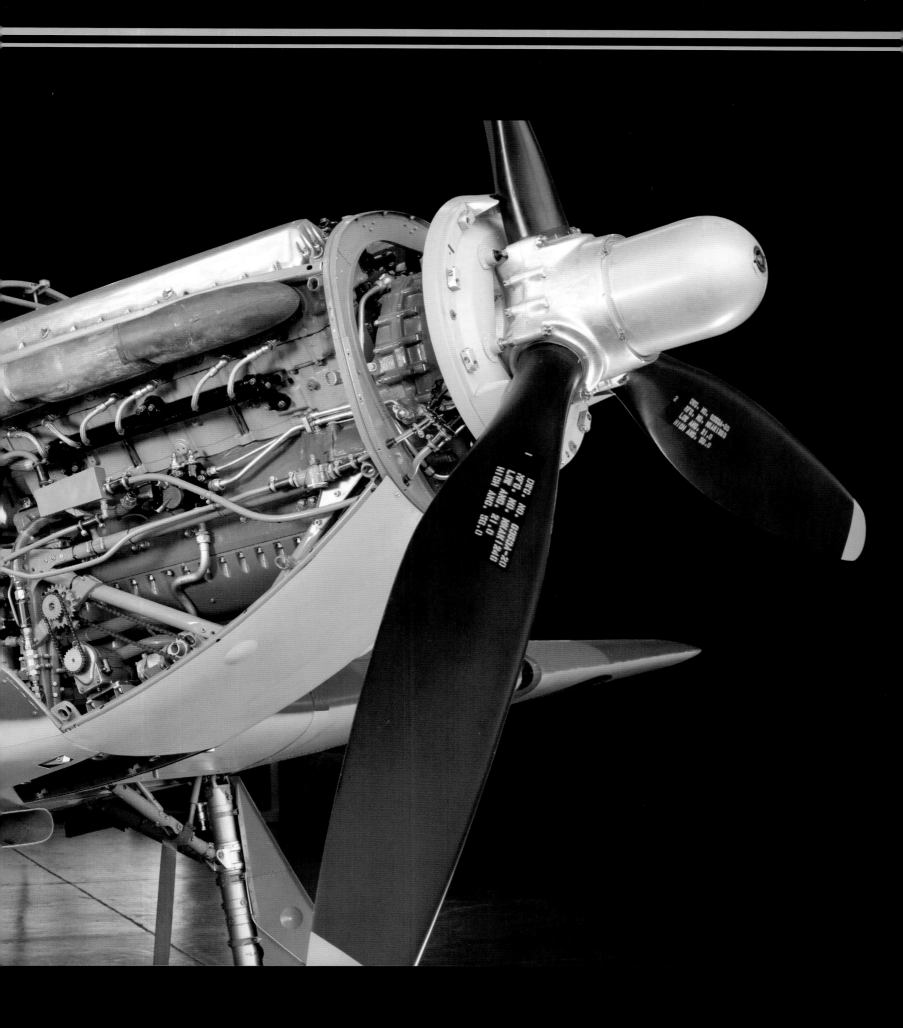

DWG. NO. 6395A-20
MFG. NO. NGAN1260
LOW ANG. 21.0
HIGH ANG. 56.0

DWG. NO. 6395A-20
MFG. NO. NGAN1260
LOW ANG. 21.0
HIGH ANG. 56.0

ABOVE: This image shows the distinctive exhaust stacks of the Hurricane's Merlin engine. Many think the name Merlin came from the King Arthur legend. However, Rolls-Royce chose the names of birds of prey for their power plants—Falcon, Eagle, and Buzzard. The merlin is a small hawk seen in the northern hemisphere.

OPPOSITE: The Hurricane's big, convex rear view mirror can be seen in this image of the fighter's cockpit. Note that the plane's gunsight has been removed. Sometimes, for Fly Day performances, pilots prefer to operate the planes without the space-consuming sight installed.

retractable landing gear and a fully-enclosed canopy. Both of these improvements over the Fury biplane would soon pay dividends in World War II combat theaters where the Hurricane operated from some of the most unforgiving and primitive airfields around the globe.

Spin tests of early model Hurricanes led designers to add a slightly enlarged rudder and a distinctive underfin near the fighter's fixed tail wheel.

When fighting began in France, the Hurricane's original fixed-speed, two-bladed, wooden propeller became a liability. Later versions incorporated a constant speed propeller, which allowed the prop to change blade pitch to use engine power more efficiently at various settings.

The Battle of Britain was the real test of the Hurricane. While the beautiful Supermarine Spitfire stole all the headlines, the Hawker Hurricane did more of the work. Britain had more Hurricanes than Spitfires because they were much simpler to build.

In battle, German explosive bullets sometimes passed right through a Hurricane's biplane-era fabric-covered aft fuselage without detonating. And, due to the simple (some would say outdated) construction method, the metal tube structures and basic skins could usually be repaired fairly quickly and the Hurricane could be returned to active service much faster than a Spitfire.

When everything went as planned in the skies over Britain, there was a certain division of labor between the RAF Spitfire and Hurricane pilots. The fast and maneuverable Spitfires took on the German fighters while the Hurricanes went after the enemy bombers. The Hurricane was uniquely suited to this task: sturdy and steady as a gun platform, it had an ample wing that could carry an arsenal, often eight Browning machine guns.

When the summer of 1940 was over, the Hurricane had accounted for 1,593 of the 2,739 total air-to-air victories claimed in the Battle of Britain. Though nearly obsolete, the Hurricane went on to serve in nearly every combat theater, including North Africa, Southeast Asia, the Mediterranean, and on the Eastern Front with the Soviets. As with many proven planes, the Hurricane took on more than fighter duties. Versions of the plane flew as ground attack craft, night fighters, and reconnaissance planes.

Pilots said that the Hurricane was a big and powerful, but gentle machine. From the cockpit, a flyer could see nearly everything, but was deafened by the roar of the Merlin engine and the constant drumming of the fighter's fabric-skinned sides. Where the I-16 was skittish and slippery, the Hurricane flew steady, sturdy, and solid. This characteristic was not great in a turning dogfight but was excellent for getting the maximum amount of lead into the hide of a slow-moving German bomber.

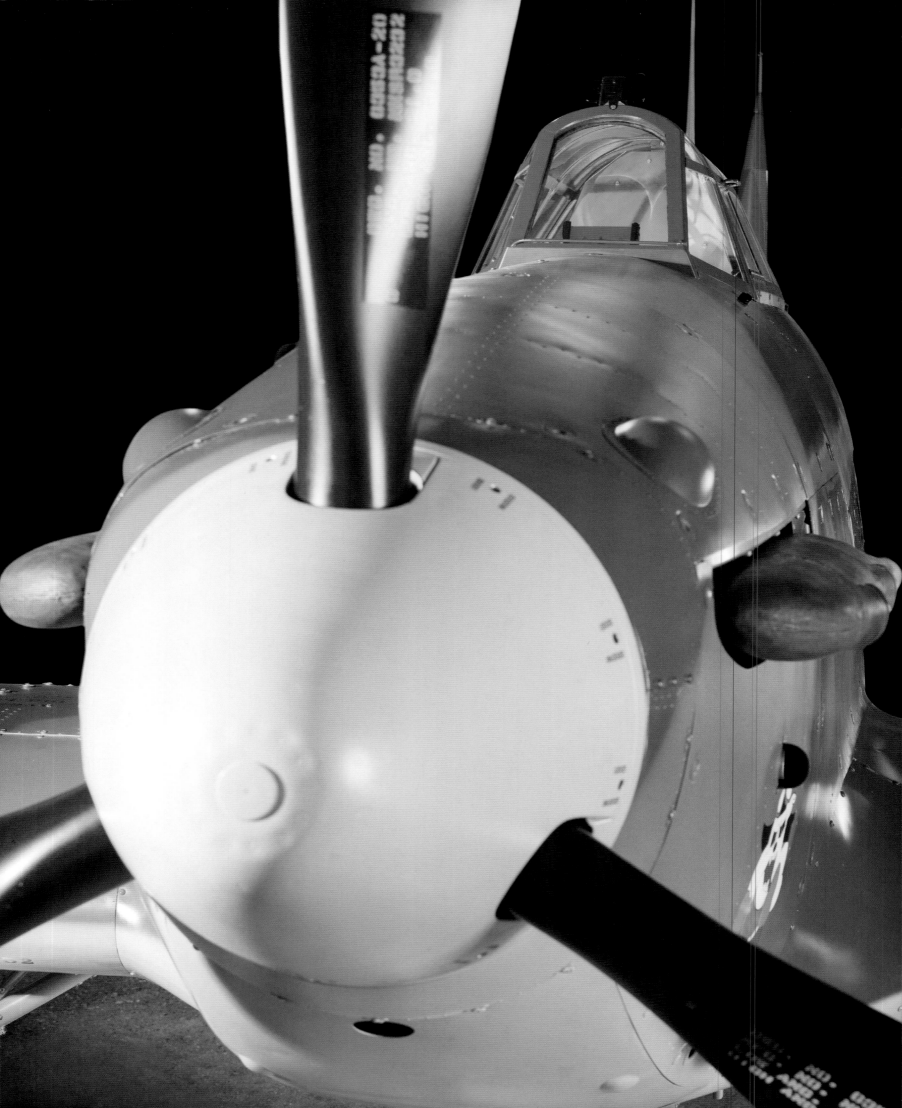

The FHC Hurricane was one of 1,451 Hurricanes built by the Canadian Car & Foundry Company (CCF) at Fort William, Ontario, Canada. The British Air Ministry, concerned about damage that could be done to aircraft factories in the UK, developed a specification for the Canadian Department of National Defense in 1939 for aircraft production in Canada. In short order, the CCF received a contract, a Hawker Hurricane to use as a pattern, and microfilm of drawings of all components and manufacturing tools. The first forty Hurricanes were produced by September 1940.

The collection's aircraft was one of a block of fifty Sea Hurricanes ordered in 1941 for use in the RAF's Merchant Ship Fighter Unit. The planes were fitted with catapult spools, slinging gear, and a naval radio to communicate with merchant ships. The FHC aircraft was built with a Merlin III engine, a three-bladed de Havilland Hamilton Hydromatic propeller, and eight .303-inch machine guns. Serial number BW 881 was delivered to Eastern Air Command at Dartmouth, Nova Scotia, on January 22, 1942. No. 118 (F) Fighter Squadron took charge of this aircraft, but it was seconded to the Admiralty in Halifax, stored for possible use. The aircraft never saw active service with the Merchant Ship Fighter Unit.

On June 23, 1943, the FHC's aircraft was returned to the CCF where it was converted to a Mk.XIIA. This version used an American-built Packard Merlin XXIX engine. After conversion, the aircraft was transferred to No. 1 (F) Operation Training Unit at Bagotville, Quebec in September 1943. A few weeks later, the Hurricane had just taken off and was climbing through four thousand feet, near St. Anne, Quebec, when its engine quit. Flight Sergeant E. E. Whitehead guided the plane down to a belly landing and was uninjured in the crash. The plane was judged Category D (damage pertaining to power plant). Investigation placed the cause of the failure on "engine threw oil through the breather . . . Possibility scavenge pump failed."

Slightly less than a year later, on September 7, 1944, the Hurricane was involved in a Category B (not repairable on site) crash at Chicoutimi, Quebec. The report on the accident states that Flight Officer E. L. Banks was testing a new engine that quit due to a broken connecting rod. Banks brought the plane down for a wheels-up landing "behind Chicoutimi hospital." He was uninjured in the crash but the plane was heavily damaged. It was transferred to the No. 9 Repair Depot on September 9, 1944 but there is no indication that any work was carried out.

ABOVE: The prototype Hawker Hurricane first took to the skies in 1935 with H.G. Hawker Engineering's Chief Test Pilot, Flight Lt. Paul Ward Spencer "George" Bulman in the cockpit. Tests with the plane led to many improvements in the Hurricane's design, most notably the addition of an underfin and all-metal stressed Duralumin wings.

OPPOSITE: The FHC's Hurricane has one thing the aircraft of RCAF No. 135 Squadron did not—a spinner. The squadron's planes flew with an American engine and propeller and the prop dome was too big to cover the original style spinner. So, through most of the war, No. 135 planes flew without the streamlined piece of metal at the nose of the aircraft.

On September 28, 1944, the aircraft was written off to "spares and produce."

The ensuing history of the FHC Hurricane is not entirely clear; however, it appears that Cameron Logan, a farmer in Quebec, purchased the remains of the aircraft after the war. The wreck sat at his farm in Saint-Jean-sur-Richelieu for thirty-five years before Jack Arnold, an aviation collector in Brantford, Ontario, purchased it in 1982. Passed through many hands, the Hurricane wreck became the property of the Alpine Fighter Collection of New Zealand in 1998.

The FHC acquired the Hurricane as part of a four-aircraft deal with the Alpine in August of that year. The Hurricane was restored at Hawker Restorations in Milden, England. Hawker Restorations specializes in the rebuilding of Hurricanes, and has acquired and developed the manuals, drawings, jigs, and tooling necessary to rebuild this complex airframe.

ABOVE: Gear down, the FHC's Hawker Hurricane prepares to land. The plane is a rarity—built in Canada. Since it was built in North America, the plane is equipped with a Packard Merlin engine instead of a British-built Rolls-Royce.

LEFT: The ports holding the Hurricane's Browning .303s are taped over. In combat, tape kept out dirt and moisture that might foul the weapons. As well, the tape (often red or yellow) acted as a warning to everyone working around the fighter that the guns were loaded and ready to fire.

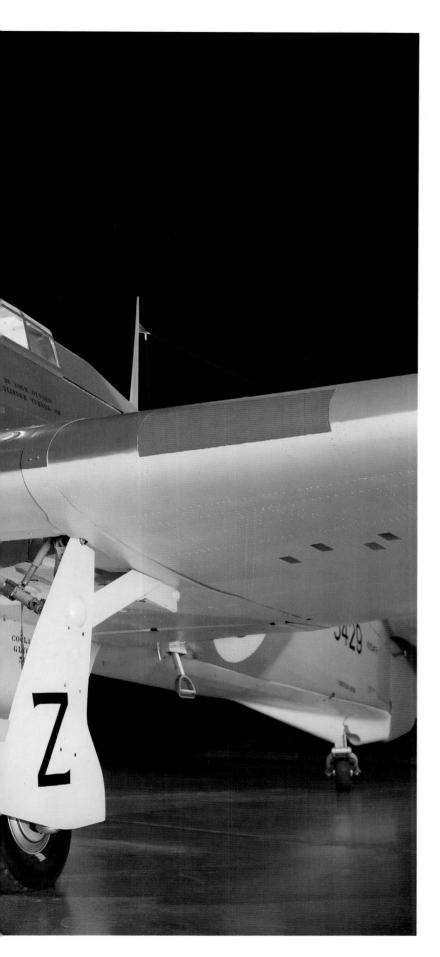

The restored BW 881 is today fitted with a Packard Merlin 224 and a Hamilton Standard hydromatic propeller. It is painted with the colors of the Canadian Home Defense No. 135 (F) Squadron. The "Bulldog Squadron" was assigned to the Western Air Command, headquartered in Vancouver, British Columbia. The 135th was formed at Mosabank, Saskatchewan, and eventually moved to Patricia Bay, British Columbia; Annette Island, Alaska; and Terrace, British Columbia. The bulldog emblem was inspired by the squadron's mascot, a bulldog named "King."

The fully restored Hurricane was first flight tested by Stuart Goldspink in England before being shipped to Arlington, Washington, in August 2006. It was reassembled after arrival in Arlington and is today flown regularly at Fly Day events at the FHC in Everett, Washington.

Amazingly, the FHC's rare Bf 109 E-3 was brought back from the dead. After it
was lost during the Battle of Britain, it was painstakingly rebuilt for years by
expert restorers.

THE
RIVALS

MESSERSCHMITT BF 109 E-3

SUPERMARINE SPITFIRE F.MK.VC

Before World War II, the German Messerschmitt Bf 109 and the Vickers Supermarine Spitfire were two of the world's fastest, most capable fighter aircraft. Both were products of the first wave of monoplane fighter development in the mid-1930s and both were exceptional designs. Undoubtedly most famous for their clashes during the Battle of Britain, the two rivals remained in a seesaw battle for superiority during much of the war.

The pair had much in common while being quite different. The Spitfire and Bf 109 were both the result of great leaps in aero engine technology coupled with corresponding improvements in airframe design, which allowed fighters' structure to handle this massive jump in horsepower. The introduction of these aircraft, along with the Hawker Hurricane, made it clear that the days of the biplane fighter were definitively over. Tight turning and intricate maneuvers were no longer the things that won air battles. Now, it was blistering speed combined with brutal firepower.

The two planes were built as compact, spry interceptors. As much as a frontline warplane can be called a defensive weapon, these fighters fit the bill. They did not carry much fuel or have roomy cockpits for long escort flights. They were meant to hotrod into the skies at a moment's notice to meet an oncoming threat. As the war progressed and roles changed, designers in both Germany and Great Britain worked to keep these fighters effective by rolling out different and improved versions of these trusty machines.

ABOVE: A keen observer will notice one extra addition to the FHC's Bf 109—the cable near the tail wheel holds the controls for a tail wheel lock. In order to safely operate this ultra-rare fighter, pilots lock the tail wheel into position on takeoff and landing.

Let's first look at the development of the German fighter. Amazingly, the famous Bf 109 was the first combat aircraft from *Bayerische Flugzeugwerke* (Bavarian Aircraft Company and hence the Bf moniker). Willy Messerschmitt was at odds with some of Germany's top military brass, so the 109 had to prove itself time and again in order to make it to the production stage.

Interestingly, the promised and powerful German aero engines were not available when the airframe was ready in 1935, so the first Bf 109 flew with an English-built Rolls-Royce Kestrel V-12. However, most production versions flew with Daimler-Benz 601 and 605 inverted V-12 supercharged engines.

The construction of this fighter was quite different from the contemporary Hawker Hurricane, in that the plane had very little fabric or wood incorporated into the fuselage or wings. The Bf 109 was an all-metal aircraft with monocoque construction. Instead of a steel or wooden frame at its core, the 109 had light metal structural members held in place by the outer shell of its stressed skin.

The aircraft was a cantilever, low-wing monoplane with retractable landing gear and an enclosed canopy. The one vestige of earlier times and construction styles was the supporting strut under each horizontal tail plane on early versions of the plane up through the E-model.

The Bf 109's wings were small, which meant the aircraft had high wing loading. Wing loading is a function of weight divided by wing area, and this was a trait that gave many veteran

Me 109

LEFT: A wartime era drawing shows the Allies' impression of the inner workings of their deadliest foe. This drawing helped American and British pilots identify the infamous Bf 109 in the air.

German pilots, being ex-biplane flyers, pause. Messerschmitt ignored the German Air Ministry's recommendations on wing loading and went small. Consequently, the Bf 109 performed best at high speeds and high altitudes.

One attribute that helped the Bf 109 at the other end of the performance spectrum was its leading edge slats. At high angles of attack and/or slow maneuvering speeds, the slats deployed automatically, which changed the flow of air over the top of the wing and delayed a stall. This was cutting edge technology for fighters in the mid-1930s.

By the late 1930s, the Bf 109 was really the only significant fighter in the Luftwaffe. Not only was it a stellar performer in the air, the plane could be built fairly simply and inexpensively by semi-skilled labor. The Messerschmitt Bf 109 remains the most-produced fighter aircraft of all time, with over 34,800 built.

The Spanish Civil war gave the Luftwaffe the first chance to test the Bf 109 in combat. The German Condor Legion supported the Nationalist faction in Spain and it was here that the Bf 109 first encountered the Soviet-built I-16 "Rata" flown by Republican forces. Even back then, it was hardly a fair fight. The Messerschmitt fighter simply outclassed the I-16.

The war in Spain allowed designers to perfect the finer points of the Bf 109 fighter. The conflict also allowed a core group of German flyers to gain valuable combat experience. This "practice" was needed because the 109 was never an easy plane to master and fly effectively. One outstanding danger came from the plane's narrow-track main landing gear. A significant percentage of the Bf 109s lost in wartime came from failed landings and takeoffs, not from bullets or bombs. The 109's torque-prone engine and slippery tail wheel gave novice flyers fits and a moment's inattention could be fatal.

Still, in the air, the 109 was nearly unbeatable in the hands of a skilled pilot. In Spain, then Poland, then France, Luftwaffe flyers steamrolled any aircraft they encountered. It would be the same over Russia later in the war. In fact, the only aircraft that was a match for the 109 early in the war was Great Britain's Supermarine Spitfire.

The FHC's Bf 109 actually tangled with Spitfires during the Battle of Britain and lost. The plane was built, as one of a block of 484 aircraft, at *Erla Maschinenwerk GmbH.* near Leipzig, Germany between August 1939 and May 1940.

After construction, it was released to the Luftwaffe. Very few records have been discovered on this aircraft and it is quite possible that the plane was assigned to numerous flying groups before its loss.

By the summer of 1940, the 109 had been allocated to *Staffel* ("squadron") 6 in *Jagdgeschwader* ("fighter wing") 51. The plane was assigned to Eduard Hemmerling, a twenty-seven-year-old pilot who had transferred to JG 51 from *Ergänzungs-Jagdgruppe Merseburg* in October 1939.

Hemmerling was a veteran flyer by July 1940. He was older than most in his unit and had flown with JG 51 through the French campaign. His first victory came on July 7, 1940, while escorting Do 17 bombers near Dover: he was credited with

PREVIOUS PAGES: The Messerschmitt 109's narrow landing gear stance made it very tricky to control on takeoff and landing. Some reports state that over one third of Bf 109 losses in combat theaters came from accidents, not enemy action. INSET: The emblem of JG 54 during the Battle of Britain was a cartoon crow, mocking British Prime Minister Neville Chamberlain. The slogan translates, "God punish England."

LEFT: This overhead shot shows the Bf 109's two wing-mounted 20mm MG FF cannon and its pair of nose-mounted 7.9mm MG 17 machine guns synchronized to fire through its spinning propeller.

FUEL AND FIRES

The Supermarine Spitfire and the Bf 109 both had fuel tanks directly in front of the cockpit. This positioning was great for weight and balance issues but not so good in combat. Fire from a shot-up fighter streamed directly back onto a pilot as he tried to jump out of his stricken craft. Many pilots escaped from flaming fighters with severely burned faces and hands, a condition RAF doctors called "Airman's Burn." Men like Dr. Archibald McIndoe worked for years to perfect reconstructive surgery techniques to help these flyers get on with their lives after their brush with death.

RIGHT: The BF 109's exhaust stacks and valve covers are at the bottom, while the crankshaft is located at the top of the engine block. Though an inverted V engine seems odd to many, the arrangement had certain advantages— it kept the engine's center of gravity low and allowed for better visibility over the nose of the fighter.

shooting down a Spitfire. Just two days later, Hemmerling attacked and destroyed a 40 Squadron Bristol Blenheim light bomber near Cap Gris Nez on the northern coast of France.

In the early hours of July 29, 1940, a group of about 130 German aircraft headed across the English Channel to attack a convoy of ships near Dover. Around forty-eight *Stuka* dive-bombers were escorted by a large complement of Bf 109s from various fighter units. Spitfires from 41 and 64 Squadrons, as well as Hurricanes from 501 and 56 Squadrons, were scrambled to meet the oncoming attackers.

In the fight, Hemmerling, in the FHC's aircraft, was observed to shoot down a British fighter, most likely a Spitfire.

RIGHT: Two US fighter pilots inspect a late model Messerschmitt shot down in combat. The circular shape near the bottom of the image is the plane's vertically-mounted supercharger.

BELOW: The FHC's Bf 109 E-3 is powered by a Daimler-Benz DB 601 Aa engine, generating 1,150 horsepower. The diminutive fighter could reach speeds of 357 mph at 12,300 feet.

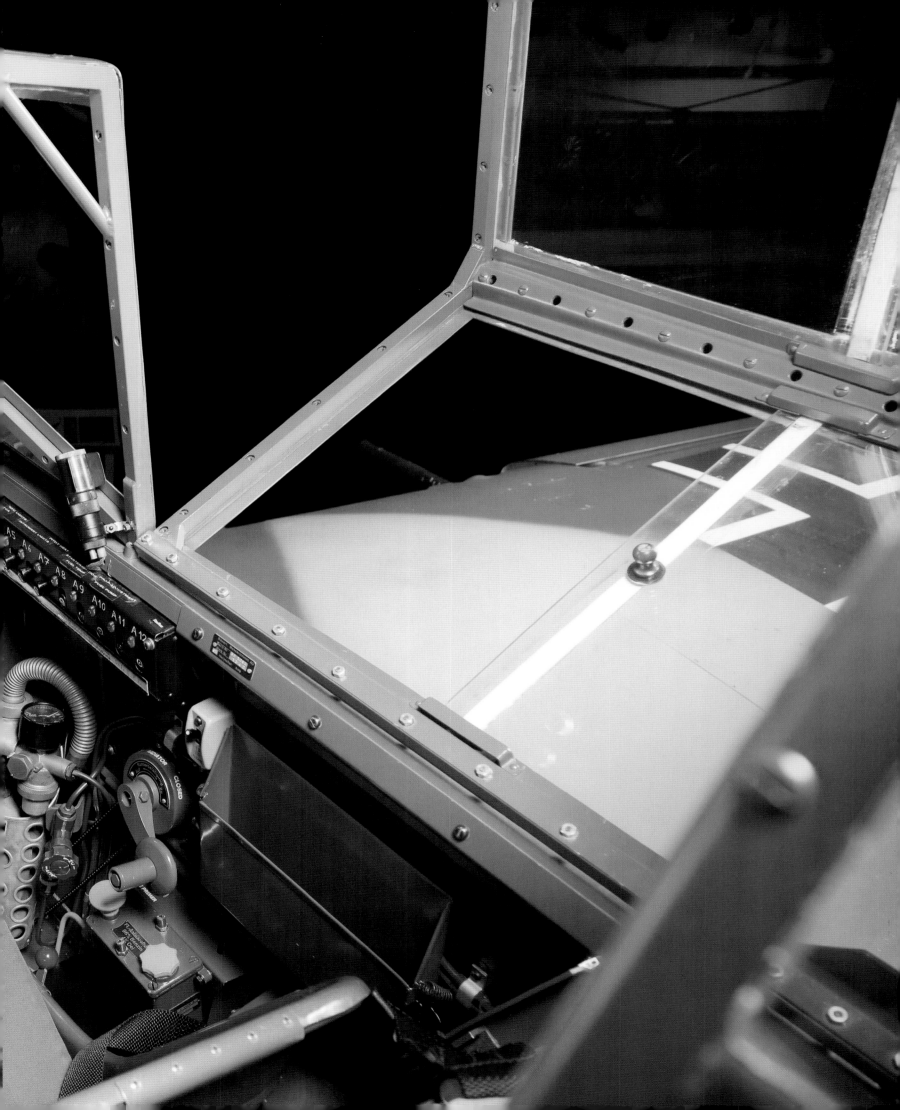

The number of aircraft lost in this engagement varies widely by source, though both sides sustained many losses—aircraft damaged, bailouts, and crash landings. Many believe Hemmerling was attacked by Flight Leader "Johnny" Webster of 41 Squadron in a Spitfire.

TOP: This grainy image was taken from a frame of a film shot during Germany's aerial attacks on Britain. The emblem on the nose is the "horrible *Tatzelwurm*,"—a mythical creature from the Alps.

ABOVE: It changes the shape of the wing and allows the Messerschmitt to handle better at the bottom end of its performance envelope.

PREVIOUS PAGES: The Bf 109's cramped cockpit was topped by faceted, flat-paned Perspex (clear plastic). The flat surfaces were much easier to produce quickly and limited distortion was seen in curved canopies.

Presumably, Hemmerling's damaged aircraft staggered away from the fight and back toward France. What happened to Hemmerling remains a mystery. His aircraft was found many years later, though there is no record of his rescue or burial. One of the most likely scenarios is that Hemmerling's plane came down in the English Channel, quite near the French coast, and the young pilot, perhaps wounded, may have died of hypothermia in the water. He may have been knocked out, or been injured in his attempt to ditch the damaged fighter.

The loss of Hemmerling was the end of the story for more than forty-five years. However, in 1988, a Frenchman discovered something in the sand while walking along the beach near Cap Blanc Nez, not far from Calais, France. It was after a strong storm, and as sometimes happens, the contours of the beach had shifted, revealing something that had been buried there for years.

What started out as a wingtip jutting from the sand, soon became most of a relatively intact German fighter plane. The plane has been described by some as whole except for a "burnt out engine," and by others, including one of the first owners, a European warbird enthusiast and wreck-chaser named Christiaan Vanhee, as only partially complete with both wings, main landing gear, and sections of the fuselage.

The airframe was briefly displayed in France before being transported to the United Kingdom for eventual restoration. By this time, the owner of the aircraft was New Zealander Sir Tim Wallis but the restoration of the Bf 109 was to be performed by Craig Charleston of Charleston Aviation Services based in Essex, England. It was only then that the plane's history came to light. Restorers discovered the *Werke Nummer*, 1342, stamped into a part on the undercarriage assembly, leading to revelations about JG 51 and Hemmerling.

Charleston's work is reputed to be some of the best—with painstaking attention to detail and the use of period hardware and equipment. Because the aircraft was going to be made flyable, the work is often called, in the press, "restoration *and* remanufacture."

The FHC acquired the Bf 109 as part of a four-aircraft deal with the Alpine Deer Group of New Zealand in August 1998. The aircraft was mated with the restored Daimler-Benz DB 601 Aa engine overhauled by Mike Nixon of Vintage V-12s Inc. of Tehachapi, California, in the last part of 2004. In January of 2005, the aircraft underwent taxi and engine tests at Wattisham, Suffolk.

ABOVE: The FHC's Supermarine Spitfire is a fan favorite on Battle of Britain Day at the FHC. Several pilots who flew Spitfires in combat have brought their families to Everett to watch "their" aircraft zoom through the skies.

The plane was subsequently shipped to the United States and was stored at Arlington, Washington, along with other aircraft in the collection. Leading up to the move of aircraft to the new Everett facility, the Bf 109 was brought back to flying condition and flown for the first time since July 29, 1940. With Craig Charleston on hand to assist in the maiden flight, warbird pilot Steve Hinton took the plane to the skies on March 22, 2008.

Today, the reborn fighter participates in the FHC's free Fly Days including, of course, Battle of Britain Day. Often, the Bf 109's main rival and nemesis flies in those performances, too.

The Supermarine Spitfire first flew slightly less than a year after the Bf 109. Aesthetically, the fighters are complete opposites. While the Messerschmitt Bf 109 is a somber mix of angles and flat planes, the Spitfire is an eye-popping spectacle of curves and sleek lines. Flyers say that "if a plane looks good, it flies good." The Spitfire was like a movie star—not only dazzling, but instantly famous too.

The Spitfire fighter was born from the Supermarine racing floatplanes of the 1920s. At the last Schneider Trophy event in 1931, the Supermarine S.6B—a six-ton floatplane—topped 340 mph. While the design of the Spitfire's airframe was a completely new creation, many of the lessons learned from the sleek, high-horsepower racers went into the soul of the new fighter plane.

Supermarine Aviation Works' chief designer R. J. Mitchell was integral to the birth of the Spitfire. Mitchell created the S.6B racer and the Type 300, the plane that would become the Spitfire. In the racing world, aerodynamics and efficiency were the keys to speed (along with, perhaps, a generous helping of horsepower). Mitchell refined the curves of his fighter over and over again, smoothing corners and perfecting lines.

Another racing trick: steal any advantage you can get, from any source. The Spitfire received a fraction of its energy from the shape and angle of its supercharged Merlin V-12 engine exhaust stacks and an additional push from hot gases escaping

ABOVE: Many Americans flew Spitfires as well. Joseph Kelly flew "Little Joe" as a member of the RAF's "Eagle Squadron"—flyers from the United States fighting for Great Britain.

PREVIOUS PAGES: The FHC's Spitfire VC is a combat veteran, damaged during a fighter mission with the RAF's No. 312 Squadron over the English Channel.

from a cleverly-designed radiator scoop. Some say harnessing this parasitic power was worth seventy horsepower at 300 mph.

The Spitfire's semi-elliptical wings accomplished two things at once. They had the characteristics and aerodynamic performance of a long span wing with many of the structural attributes normally seen in a short, stubby wing. The Spitfire had lower wing loading than the Bf 109 and excelled at lower speeds and lower altitudes than the Messerschmitt. Compared to the Hurricane, the Spitfire's wings were quite thin—just big enough to hold guns and landing gear fully enclosed in its airfoil shape.

Though the Spitfire was a great performer in the air, producing it in the factory was a nightmare. Many of the first Spitfires were almost hand-built pieces of art. The curvy

body and semi-elliptical wings, along with semi-monocoque stressed skin construction made each plane much harder to build than a "homely Hurricane." The Spitfire would become the most-produced British fighter of all time in more than forty different versions, but at the dawn of the Battle of Britain, there were many more Hurricanes on hand than Spitfires.

When the Bf 109 and Spitfire met in the skies over southern England, the pair was often quite evenly matched. Bf 109s carried 20mm cannons. At the time, Spitfires flew with only .303-caliber guns. In the swirling chaos of a dogfight, a fraction of a second in someone's sights, that single hit, could be the deciding factor. The heavier projectile did more damage when it struck home.

The Daimler-Benz engine of the Messerschmitt had fuel injection; the Spitfire's Merlin had a carburetor. It allowed Bf 109s to complete inverted and negative-g maneuvers that made the Spitfire's engine cut out.

The Bf 109 pilots usually had more combat experience than RAF flyers, however the nature and location of the fight often favored the RAF pilots. Naturally, dogfights degenerated into lower altitude, lower speed engagements—giving the advantage to a Spitfire pilot. And, Messerschmitt flyers had less time to fight before their fuel ran out and they had to return to France.

The FHC's Spitfire is a product of improvements made on Battle of Britain-era aircraft. AR614 was one of 2,158 built at the Westland Aircraft Ltd. factory in Yeovil, Somerset. The Mk.V variant, with over 6,500 built, became the most-produced version of the Spitfire. The Mk.V had more powerful cannon, a better engine, and a new carburetor design to prevent engine cutout during negative-G maneuvers. The FHC Mk.VC was built with the Merlin 46 engine, a high altitude version of the Merlin 45.

AR614 was delivered from the factory to No. 39 Maintenance Unit (MU) at Colerne on August 24, 1942. From there, in September, the aircraft went to No. 312 Squadron at Harrowbeer, Devon, which was made up of Czechoslovakian pilots who had made their way to England to continue the fight against Germany.

On November 7, 1942, after barely two months in combat service, AR614 was involved in a Category Ac accident when the port tire burst approximately one third of the way down the runway at Churchstanton. This damage was repairable onsite by another unit and the aircraft was reported back in service the day after.

continued on page 95

LEFT: The Spitfire's windscreen was made from bulletproof glass while the side panels were Perspex. Above is the Spitfire's rear view mirror—critical for spotting an attacker moving up from behind the plane.

BELOW: At sunset, the FHC's Spitfire stands with its cowls off during an annual inspection. The aircraft in the collection undergo a strict inspection and maintenance regimen to keep them in top flying shape.

ABOVE: The FHC's Spitfire carries a trio of unsightly scoops on its underside. In the center is the carburetor air inlet. The big box under the starboard wing holds the radiator. The long cylindrical scoop under the port wing houses the plane's oil cooler.

RIGHT: The Spitfire was small and compact—a trait liked by most pilots who flew it. The plane's disadvantage came from its diminutive size as well: The plane could carry only so much fuel, giving it a limited range.

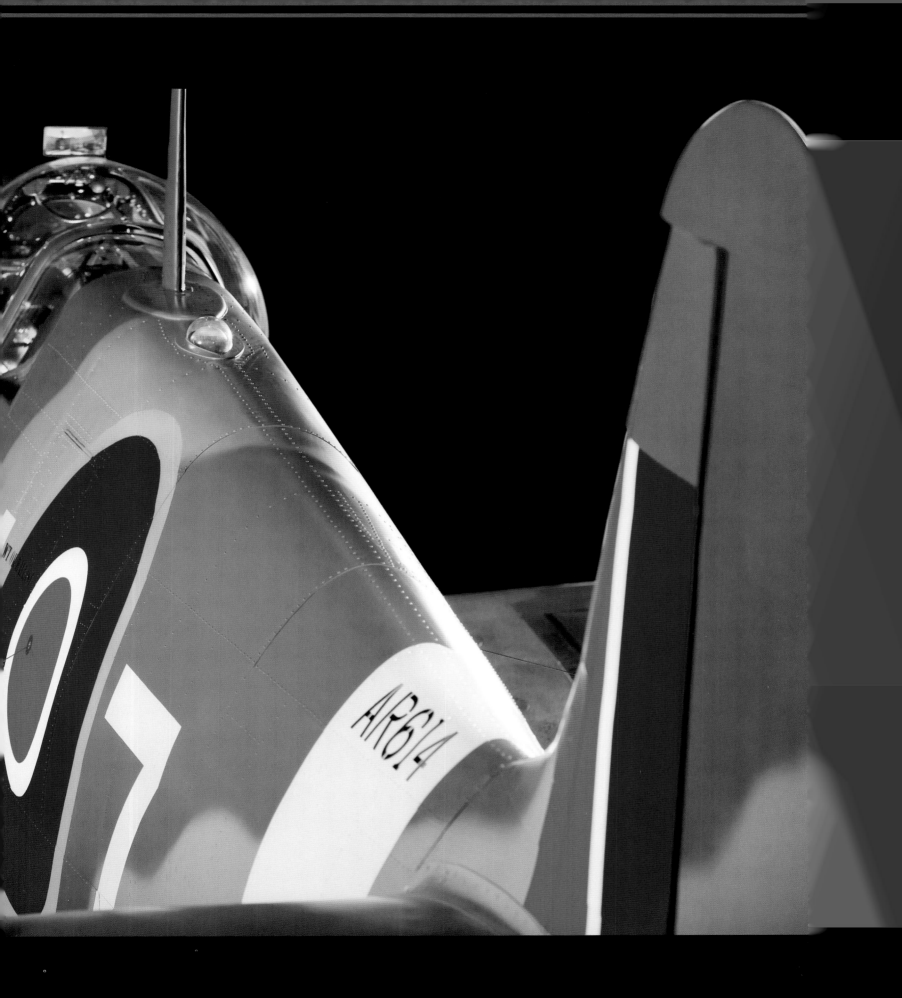

ABOVE: Yugoslavian partisans help keep RAF Spitfires up and running in Italy during combat operations. The planes in the photo are equipped with elongated chins that contain tropical filters to keep sand and dust out of the engine.

OPPOSITE: Part of the Spitfire's aesthetic appeal comes from its elliptical wings, which taper dramatically near the wingtips. Not only does it look spectacular, the wing shape minimizes induced drag, making the fighter more efficient.

RIGHT: The Spitfire's Rolls-Royce Merlin engine was the heart of the speedy fighter. The FHC exhibits an example of the 1,500 horsepower Merlin next to the collection's Spitfire, Hurricane, or P-51 Mustang. This version of the engine came from a de Havilland Mosquito fighter.

continued from page 88

The final mission for AR614 came on May 14, 1943, when Thomas Vybiral led the squadron together with No. 313 Squadron in an attack on St. Peter Port harbor, Guernsey (one of the Channel Islands near the coast of Lower Normandy, France). The operation, called "Roadstead 2," found twelve German E-boats and other small warships and merchantmen in harbor, but was met by intense flak. AR614, Vybiral's aircraft, was hit just behind the cockpit where the radio and IFF unit were knocked out. Vybiral was, however, able to lead the squadron back to base.

Afterward, AR614 participated in the "Wings for Victory" fund-raising efforts in Taunton in May 1943 before being taken for repair at an Air Service Training unit in June. In the meantime, the damage had been recoded from Category Ac to Category B (beyond repair on-site). The aircraft was sent to No. 6 Maintenance Unit at RAF Brize Norton in Oxfordshire in September 1943.

AR614 was then passed to No. 610 (County of Chester) Squadron, No. 130 (Punjab) Squadron, then No. 222 (Natal) Squadron at Catterick, Yorkshire. There, the plane suffered another Category Ac accident during flying operations on February 21, 1944, and was repaired onsite by March.

The plane returned to No. 222 Squadron, but was transferred to No. 3501 (SU) Servicing Unit in May, and then became a pilot trainer with No. 53 (OTU) Operational Training Unit at Caistor, Lincolnshire.

Barely two weeks later, AR614 suffered another Category Ac accident. It was returned to No. 53 OTU on October 13, 1944. The plane's flying career came to an end in June 1945 when it was transferred to No. 33 MU at Lyneham, Wiltshire. At this point, No. 33 MU was acting as an Aircraft Storage Unit and "by late 1946 the MU held nearly 750 aircraft . . . so a lot of the aircraft were stored tipped up onto their noses in the hangars."

In July 1945, AR614 was transferred to St. Athan, Glamorgan, Wales, and was probably used by No. 4 School of Technical Training as an instructional aircraft. During the 1950s and early 1960s, the Spitfire served as a display aircraft or gate guard at RAF Padgate, RAF West Kirby, RAF Hednesford, and RAF Bridgnorth.

LEFT: The Spitfire's designer, R. J. Mitchell, wanted his plane to be named the Supermarine Shrew. When the company picked Spitfire—an old English term for someone with a strong or fiery character—Mitchell stated that he thought the moniker was "bloody silly."

In 1963, the plane was moved to RAF Dishforth as scrap and then sold to the Air Museum in Calgary, Canada, in 1964. The plane remained in storage until the museum sold it to Donald Campbell in 1970. A report from the time quoted Campbell (Lt. P. D. Campbell, Chief Instructor of No. 647 Squadron of the Royal Canadian Air Cadets) as saying, "This may sound a little foolish, but when we heard of a 'Spitfire Mark V' that was up for grabs last fall we obtained it as well." He stored the aircraft in Kapuskasing, Ontario, until beginning restoration in late 1985.

Campbell registered the fighter in Canada as C-FDUY in 1986. The "DUY" refers to the No. 312 squadron/aircraft code letters. Campbell must have believed these to be accurate at the time the plane was registered, but he subsequently learned from the Free Czechoslovak Air Force Association that AR614 carried the code letters DU-Z.

The Old Flying Machine Company purchased the aircraft in October 1992 and moved it to Duxford for further restoration. The plane was sold to the Alpine Fighter Collection in New Zealand in May 1994. Sir Tim Wallis of Alpine Fighter Collection commissioned Historic Flying of Audley End to rebuild the aircraft, and it first flew in October 1996.

The FHC acquired the Spitfire from Alpine Deer Group in August of 1998. The collection commissioned Hawker Restorations, Ltd., to complete the restoration work. Once in the United States, the rebuilt Spitfire was registered as N614VC.

After the Battle of Britain, both the Bf 109 and Spitfire designs continued to be improved as the war continued. More range, more speed, and varied weaponry kept the aircraft potent as the seesaw battle for the preeminent fighter raged on. Messerschmitt almost completely reinvented their aircraft with the arrival of the Bf 109 F—often judged to be the best version of the 109. The last operational version of the Bf 109 was a K-4. Soon after, the Third Reich was defeated and all combat aircraft production came to an end in Germany.

Marks of Spitfires continued to come off assembly lines throughout World War II and beyond—V, then IX, up to Rolls-Royce Griffon-powered Spitfire Mk.24 and additional, more advanced naval versions of the fighter. The Spitfire outlasted the Messerschmitt, in the air and in the factories as well. The last Spitfire fighter was built in 1948 (the last Seafire, in 1949). Flying alongside jet fighters, the last of the Spitfires were retired from RAF service in 1954.

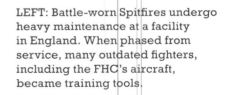

LEFT: Battle-worn Spitfires undergo heavy maintenance at a facility in England. When phased from service, many outdated fighters, including the FHC's aircraft, became training tools.

OPPOSITE: A rocker switch mounted on the control stick fired the Spitfire's guns. Pilots came up with a simple solution to memorize the tricky switch: BBC, which stood for Brownings, Both, Cannon. If a flyer hit the top of the switch, he would get machine guns only (Brownings), press the middle and all guns fired, and the bottom part of the switch activated the cannons alone.

The FHC's Curtiss P-40C Tomahawk saw combat in northwest Russia during World War II, flying and fighting in some of the most extreme conditions in the world.

DUELS IN CHINA 4

CURTISS P-40C TOMAHAWK

NAKAJIMA KI-43 *HAYABUSA*
OSCAR TYPE I

The Curtiss-Wright P-40 Hawk series of fighter planes first flew in 1938; years after the Bf 109 (1935) and Spitfire (1936) made their debuts. However, the American aircraft never matched its European counterparts. With the threat of war on the horizon, the United States Army Air Corps chose the P-40, not because it was the best, but because it could be built quickly and in great numbers. And, while the fighter was never a world-beater, it is arguably one of the most important Allied warplanes of the opening years of World War II.

The story of the P-40 starts with the radial engine powered Curtiss P-36. First flown in 1935, the Curtiss Hawk and Mohawk fighters had relatively short careers in army service and were considered obsolete by the beginning of World War II. However, the availability of an Allison in-line engine in 1937 gave potential to an improved version of the Hawk.

The P-40 was almost identical to the P-36, except for the new liquid-cooled V-12 engine in the nose. The first example flew in October 1938, and the first delivery of production planes came in May 1940. That summer, in Europe, the fighters of the RAF and Luftwaffe were locked in combat that would determine the future of Great Britain. It did not take an aeronautical engineer to see that the P-40 was not up to the standards of a Spitfire or Bf 109.

While the Curtiss P-40 was the first US fighter capable of three hundred miles per hour, it had the soul of an ancient airplane. It was slower than the Spitfire and Bf 109, had a mix of light armament, featured no self-sealing fuel tanks, and had very little armor. Toe-to-toe, early P-40s stood no chance against Europe's best.

This was not solely the fault of Curtiss. The US military got what they asked for. The P-40 was made for low altitudes and ground support operations. Curtiss did not build a plane to tussle with the best fighters of the day at higher altitudes.

ABOVE: In this touched-up Russian propaganda photo, one of America's Tomahawk fighters can be seen in service with flyers of the Soviet Air Force near Murmansk.

RIGHT: Flying Tiger aircraft were originally produced for Britain as Lend-Lease aircraft. As a result, they wear RAF-style camouflage. If you look closely at the patterns on the wings and fuselage, you can see the outline of spots where the British roundels were supposed to be placed.

ABOVE: Uncowled for inspection, the P-40's "long-nose" Allison engine can be seen. The C-model power plant had an extended gear reduction case that helped it fit into streamlined fighters like the Curtiss Tomahawk.

The fighter, like the P-36 before it, was a low-wing, all-metal monoplane with an enclosed cockpit and retractable landing gear—typical for the mid to late 1930s. It featured an Alclad skin (corrosion-resistant aluminum sheet made by Alcoa Inc.) with flush rivets. The wings were National Advisory Committee for Aeronautics (NACA) aerofoil 2215 at the root and 2209 near the tip. The initial version of the plane carried four .30-caliber machine guns in its wings and two .50-caliber machine guns in its nose. One distinctive feature of the plane was its main landing gear, which retracted backward and rotated through ninety degrees to lie flat within the wing.

Even with shortcomings, there was urgent demand for the P-40. The plane could be built immediately and in great numbers. Curtiss got the green light to make as many P-40s as they could and improvements would happen on the fly. As problems were corrected—with additional guns, more armor, and self-sealing fuel tanks, and weight added—the plane's performance dropped even more.

Great Britain, fighting in the skies over Africa, took what they could get. France, about to be overrun by German Panzers, wanted the P-40s too. Later, Russia would use the planes at low level to attack the invading German armies and wanted squadrons of the American machines.

China also wanted the P-40s. The Nationalist Chinese, fighting the Japanese, needed modern weapons and skilled pilots to turn the tide. American military pilots, led by ex-army aviator Claire Chennault, resigned their commissions and volunteered to go to China along with a hundred Curtiss P-40B-type fighters. The American Volunteer Group (AVG), better known as the "Flying Tigers," fought alongside Chiang Kai-shek's Chinese forces.

The AVG's P-40s, adorned with their famous shark mouths, fared well against Japanese Nate and Oscar fighters. Chennault insisted that his pilots play to the P-40's strengths. Above all, he warned, avoid low-speed turning fights against the more maneuverable Japanese types that the P-40s could not win. It was always "hit and run" with the Curtiss planes. Dive in, attack, and climb away at high speed to set up another pass. According to the Flying Tigers Association, the Flying Tigers shot down 299 Japanese aircraft while losing just 12 planes in combat.

The P-40 was the primary US Army fighter when the Japanese attacked Pearl Harbor. It fought in Hawaii, the Philippines, Alaska, Africa, and Southern Europe—nearly everywhere. However, never equipped for high altitude escort work, P-40s did not fly combat missions from England.

Another reason the P-40 was kept out of the fights over the English Channel and beyond was that the plane was always outclassed by the latest Bf 109. American pilots in Africa and Italy had a little joke about meeting a Messerschmitt while piloting a P-40. "You might as well stay and fight," they said, "because you certainly can't run away."

One trait nearly every P-40 pilot agreed upon was that the plane was rugged. It could be flown from extremely primitive airfields and it could absorb tremendous punishment and return home safely.

As the P-47 and P-51 arrived in greater numbers, P-40s were withdrawn from frontline service. More Curtiss fighters were sent to other nations while others became stateside training aircraft. Some historians complain that the P-40 was not phased out fast enough. The last of over 13,700 Curtiss P-40s was built in December 1944.

The Flying Heritage Collection P-40C Tomahawk was built in Buffalo, New York, in March 1941. The plane was one

FOLLOWING PAGES: The imposing sharkmouth was the iconic image of the American Volunteer Group. But did you know the famous Flying Tigers were actually copycats? The American airman saw the striking motif in *Illustrated Weekly of India*. It was RAF pilots fighting in North Africa that first applied the teeth and wild eyeballs to the cowls of their P-40 fighters. INSET: During its combat career, the FHC's P-40 was peppered with bullets. Restorers patched most of the holes, but left one. Pierced through the forward former just above the access door support rod, one small-caliber bullet hole remains in the veteran fighter plane.

TOP: On a test flight, the FHC's Tomahawk is put through its paces. The fighter is one of the most popular in the collection. The plane is particularly liked by children, who are drawn to its wicked sharkmouth smile.

ABOVE: A pilot helps armorers load ammunition into the wings of a Curtiss P-40 Warhawk. The flyer (on the right) is Robert Scott Jr., future author of the famous book, *God is My Co-Pilot*.

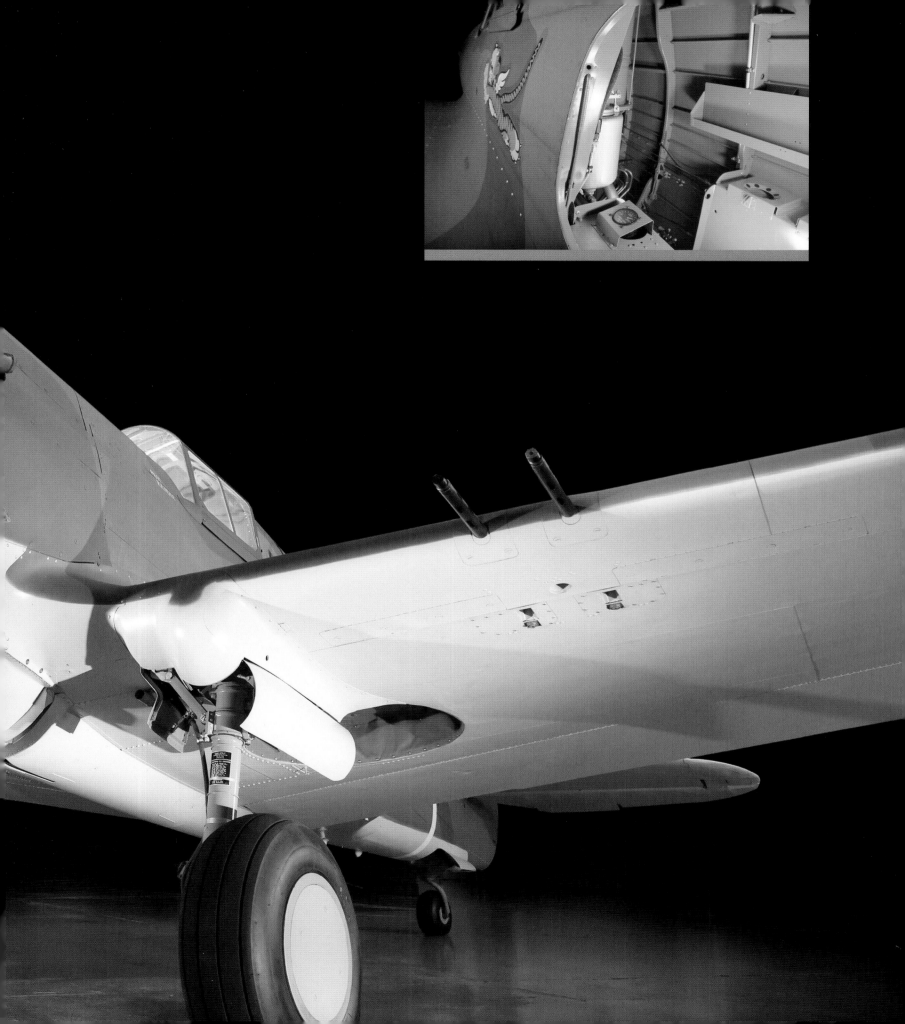

WHAT'S IN A NAME?

Both the P-40 and Ki-43 "Oscar" have stories behind their names.

The P-40 was a souped-up version of the Curtiss P-36 Hawk, which was called "Mohawk" in the United Kingdom. All versions of the P-40 had the word "hawk" in their nicknames, too. The names often depended on who was flying the aircraft. Technically, the fighters were all Warhawks when they left the factory—the American name for the P-40 fighter—but planes destined to go to the United Kingdom received different names. Early versions of the P-40 became the "Tomahawk." The P-40D-model and beyond were called "Kittyhawk" when they flew with the RAF overseas.

The FHC's Oscar has an odd, double name. The Japanese knew the Nakajima Ki-43 as "*Hayabusa*," literally Peregrine Falcon. This beautiful bird of prey, *Falco peregrinus*, is seen throughout much of the world.

Oscar was simply the Allied radio code word for the Ki-43 fighter. The military gave Japanese fighters male names like "Oscar," "Pete," "George," and "Frank," while bombers received female names such as "Val," "Betty," and "Kate." With these distinctive code names, a pilot could talk quickly and clearly about an enemy aircraft in a sort of shorthand slang.

The famous "Flying Tiger" insignia on the side of the plane is one of hundreds of designs and logos churned out by Walt Disney Studios for the military during World War II. Just like the original, the FHC's tiger decal is affixed to the plane with varnish.

of a block of 193 fighters acquired by the US Government for around $40,148.00 each. Air Corps serial number 41-13390 was built with an Allison V-1710-33 engine.

By June, the fighter had become property of the Office of Defense Aid and slated to be shipped to Europe, part of a purchase of 1,180 Curtiss fighters destined for Great Britain. Most of the planes in the batch were Tomahawk Mk.IIb aircraft straight from the Curtiss factory, equivalent to the P-40C but made specifically for Britain. Fighters of this type fought in North Africa with the RAF and South African Air Force, while others went to China and served with the famous "Flying Tigers."

Either before the P-40C ever got to England or shortly after it arrived, the Curtiss fighter was one of about 247 turned over to the Soviet Union.

The first of the Tomahawks began arriving in Russia in September 1941. The Russians were not pleased with their new aircraft. The engines were failing at a furious rate, leading many of the pilots to crash-land their new aircraft. A faulty generator drive gear "killed" nineteen engines by November 1941. For a time, the Russians grounded their P-40s to fix the issue.

The FHC's P-40 reportedly arrived at the port of Murmansk, Russia, in early 1942. The US Army P-40C, which was not an English plane with an RAF serial, caused some paperwork issues. Instead of an RAF serial, the plane number was assigned using the last three digits of its Curtiss company construction number, becoming "194."

The Russians considered the P-40s to be not as good as the Hurricane or P-39. However, it was fairly easy to fly for an average pilot. They also liked the fact that the Curtiss planes were durable—able to withstand clumsy landings and forced wheels-up crashes that were inevitably part of the pilot learning process.

Mechanically, they were a bit of a nightmare for the Russians. Besides the faulty engine parts, the Russians had no documentation besides a few worn English manuals, which they translated each night using a dictionary. There were no real spare parts or engines, leading the Russians to mix parts from damaged planes to make as many serviceable fighters as possible.

ABOVE: An interesting feature of the P-40 is its main landing gear. Upon retraction, the legs swing aft and rotate 90-degrees, allowing the plane's wheels to sit flat within the wing.

RIGHT: A US Army Curtiss P-40 comes in for landing at an airfield in China. Note that the plane is flying with part of a cowling borrowed from another Tomahawk, giving the fighter two sets of eyes.

ABOVE: The P-40 wears the insignia of the Nationalist Chinese forces. Though it is not the politest way to describe it, the American men who joined the Flying Tigers were, by definition, mercenaries.

Also, the planes were found unsuitable for Russia's terribly low temperatures. Below minus thirty-eight degrees Celsius, oil, hydraulics, even antifreeze, froze. This prompted the mechanics to install special petcocks on the planes to fully drain the liquids at night. One group of aircraft had thirty-eight burst radiators, leading mechanics to confiscate all the silverware from a nearby town for solder repairs. Batteries exploded, tires ripped on the frozen ground, and various other parts broke constantly.

The FHC plane was assigned to the 147 IAP VVS 14 Army (147th Fighter Regiment, Fourteenth Army). This group flew P-40s and Lend-Lease Hurricanes.

Aircraft 194 ran into trouble with Sr. Lt. N. V. Jurilin at the controls on February 5, 1942. The engine quit and the pilot had to belly-land the plane near Murmansk. The pilot was unhurt, but the plane was considered thirty to fifty percent damaged. Other aircraft became donors to 194, which received a new engine and many other parts from British Tomahawk IIb aircraft. While the P-40 was out of service, the 147 IAP became the 20 GIAP (20th Guards Fighter Regiment). The plane returned to the front lines on July 12, 1942.

One flyer in the 20 GIAP had participated in an amazing mission before the FHC aircraft returned to service. Flight commander Lt. Aleksey Khlobystov had rammed two Messerschmitts with his Tomahawk and lived to tell the tale.

OPPOSITE: As Germany and Great Britain fought it out in the air in Europe, it became clear that American fighters needed more protection for their pilots. Here you can see a heavy slab of armored glass that was added to the windscreen of the Tomahawk as a quick fix.

Using his right wing, the wing without the pitot tube, he had overtaken a group of Bf 110s and severed the tail of one, sending it spinning to the ground. He had then passed an attacking Bf 109 head-on, hitting it with the same right wing tip. It crashed too. Khlobystov's plane carried the tactical number "58."

The FHC's plane was found with the number "53" on its fuselage. According to writer Valeriy Romanenko, it also showed repair work done to its wing tip, presumably after a ramming attack. Today, no evidence of ramming attacks is readily apparent on the aircraft.

On the afternoon of September 27, 1942, Russian flying units in the area were attacked by around eighteen German Bf 109s. Various groups in the area fielded five Hurricanes, a P-39, and nine P-40s to intercept. The latter were from the 20 GIAP, and the FHC P-40 was among them. The planes met at altitudes of four to five thousand meters. In the dogfights that followed, the Russians claimed to have destroyed three Bf 109s for the loss of four Soviet aircraft: a Hurricane shot down; another Hurricane crash-landed; a P-40 from which the pilot bailed out; and the loss of aircraft 194, the FHC plane.

BELOW: Many Japanese aircraft wore distinctive yellow wing leading edges so that pilots could sort friend from foe in a split second.

Major Ermakov, flying 194, belly-landed his aircraft in the snow. The crash did very little damage to the plane besides crumpling the nose and the leading edges of the wings. The pilot, or others appear to have taken the plane's radio and left the scene. The aircraft sat relatively undisturbed in that remote location for fifty years.

It was found in the bleak Russian landscape in the early 1990s with the use of satellite photography. Upon investigation, the plane showed evidence of small caliber bullet damage to the tail and wings, as well as a "fresh" wound to the fighter's oil tank—the probable reason for the crash during that last combat. The aircraft, however, was almost completely intact, including its machine guns.

It was lifted from the site by helicopter and shipped to the United Kingdom where it was eventually purchased by Patina Ltd. and The Fighter Collection at Duxford. They, in turn, sent the aircraft to Fighter Rebuilders in Chino, California for restoration in 1993.

By late 1998, the fighter flew for the first time after the full restoration, with Steve Hinton at the controls. The plane was given a semi-permanent "Hollywood" paint scheme of Flying Tigers pilot Erik Schilling in anticipation of a visit by the veteran flyer. Schilling wrote later on his website: "Last Friday, I

had a most pleasant surprise. There in front of the [Planes of Fame] hangar sat a beautiful P-40C, perfect in every detail. A flood of memories rushed through my mind reminding me of the wonderful Flying Tiger days of some 57 years ago. Memories that had faded almost into obscurity were now awakened. It was almost like yesterday, as I stared at the awesome beauty of the P-40, and in my mind's eye I started reliving the experience of Burma and China. Standing there and looking at the Curtiss Hawk, I'm convinced it was the prettiest fighter ever built."

The P-40C was purchased by the FHC in March 1999. In mid-2011, the temporary paint scheme was removed and a permanent AVG paint scheme was applied. The plane now represents "Number 7" of the 1st Pursuit Squadron, which was flown by Robert H. Neale, a Seattle resident who became the AVG's top scoring ace with thirteen air-to-air victories.

The Nakajima Ki-43 Oscar was designed as a replacement for the Ki-27 army fighter, a fixed-gear monoplane that first flew in 1936. Western designers often ignored Japanese aircraft and engine designs, believing them to be poor copies of European and American creations. However, they had to admit the Nakajima Ki-27 was an exception that would soon, briefly, become the rule. The completely indigenous Ki-27 was as good, if not better, than many contemporary fighters of the era.

The Japanese Army Air Force (JAAF) soon wanted to take the next step in the evolution of this fighter design but the proposed new fighter would live in the shadow of the old. The JAAF wanted an interceptor/escort that was comparable or, preferably, superior to the Ki-27 in every way—speed, maneuverability, climb rate, and range. It assigned the task to *Nakajima Hikoki K.K.* and its engineer Hideo Itokawa.

Itokawa envisioned a plane that would be thinner and longer than the pudgy Ki-27. The new aircraft would be quite similar in construction to contemporary fighters of the time—an all-metal, low-wing, cantilever monoplane with stressed skin and an enclosed cockpit. The real difficulty for designers centered on improving both the speed *and* maneuverability

ABOVE RIGHT: The less unneeded equipment a plane hauled around, the better it performed in a dogfight. One example of spartan design in the Oscar was the "pilot's pull." A simple metal cord with a woven leather covering helped a flyer climb the plane's steep wing. It was more primitive than a stirrup or foothold, but it worked—and it weighed next to nothing.

ABOVE: The Oscar's Type 89 gunsight had a long shaft down its side that was attached to the bullet-shaped nosecone. During hours of flying, the cone helped keep the sight's lens free of oil and dirt. A pilot could turn a lever in the cockpit which rotated the sight's cover out of the way for combat.

over the Ki-27. In simple terms, one could be increased, but only at the expense of the other.

From the beginning, Itokawa planned to use the latest and most powerful Nakajima radial engine and integrate a fully retractable main landing gear. The Ki-43 would be faster than the Ki-27, of this there was no doubt. He gave the fighter a big wing and low wing loading to maximize maneuverability. The JAAF's specifications did not demand self-sealing fuel tanks, pilot armor, or the need for heavy armament—by omitting these items, the plane could stay nimble in the skies.

The first test flights of the new plane in 1939 brought disappointment. The Ki-43 was lethargic compared to the Ki-27, and some suggested abandoning the project and sticking with the older aircraft. Others wanted to lock the landing gear down permanently. Designers responded with slightly longer wings and, most importantly, a revised flap system.

One of the Ki-43's most distinctive features is the "combat flap." Nicknamed "butterfly flaps" by American observers, the paddle-shaped flaps could be deployed while the fighter was in flight, creating more lift, a tighter turn rate, and improved

ABOVE: An American soldier shot this image of an Oscar abandoned at an island airfield. It appears GIs have already started to chop out pieces of the fighter's skin to take home as souvenirs.

PREVIOUS PAGES: The FHC's Oscar is the only Type I Nakajima Ki-43 left in the world today. Visitors often confuse the Japanese army plane with its contemporary, the A6M Zero naval fighter. INSET: This image shows the FHC's Oscar the day it was captured by Australian soldiers in 1945. After suffering damage to its engine and propeller, Japanese mechanics had secreted it away into the jungle to make repairs.

flight control response. When the pilots of the AVG encountered Ki-43s over China, which they often thought were Zero fighters, they avoided getting into a turning match with the lighter more agile Japanese plane and its revolutionary flaps. To ignore Claire Chennault's doctrine was suicide.

Brilliant range, climb rate, and turning ability came at a steep price to a Japanese pilot at the controls of a Ki-43. Lack of protection and light armament made the Oscar's encounters with powerful American fighters equipped with heavy .50-caliber guns an often fatal experience. Newer models of the Ki-43 attempted to rectify some of the fighter's weaknesses, but the existing airframe allowed no room for the wholesale changes that would have made the plane significantly more competitive. During the first six months of the war in the Pacific, the Oscar was almost always outclassed.

The Ki-43 served the JAAF through the end of the war, though it was often the underdog. By 1945, many of the planes were being used as advanced trainers while others took on the job of suicide aircraft as Allied navies closed in on the home islands of Japan.

The FHC Oscar is a very rare fighter—the only surviving Ki-43 Type I in the world. The plane was the 650th Oscar produced. Little is known about the fighter between the time it left Japan in November 1942 and ended up on Rabaul. It was most likely dispatched to Truk, in the Caroline Islands, and then used to reinforce the 1st or 11th Sentai, both of which moved to Rabaul in late 1942, or early 1943.

The plane spent most of 1943 and 1944 in combat operations, before suffering a failed landing at Vunakanau Airfield on Rabaul sometime in 1945. The Oscar had a damaged engine and propeller and, due to increased pressure from American bombing units in the area, it was transported miles away from the runways and hidden among the trees for a prolonged series of repairs.

Royal Australian Air Force (RAAF) personnel occupied the area after the war. In September 1945, RAAF Squadron Leader Dennis Hamilton heard rumors of a nearly intact Oscar in the area and decided to locate it. His diary states: "We searched for aircraft in good condition, but only found some almost hidden now by the growth and all have been stripped of usable parts. An Oscar had been assembled some 3 or 4 miles from the strip and will have to be dismantled and reassembled at the strip, the whole operation taking about a week to complete.

"The location of the Army Repair unit is very carefully

ABOVE: Studying fuzzy black and white photos of the Oscar, restorers decided the chevrons on the rear fuselage must be white. When Japanese vets began to visit the project in New Zealand, they told the builders that they recalled the chevrons being yellow. Soon after, the color of the markings were changed.

RIGHT: A distinctive trait of early model Oscars was their intricate annular oil cooler mounted in front of their radial engines. Later versions of the plane had an additional scoop and a less complex cooler located inside the cowling.

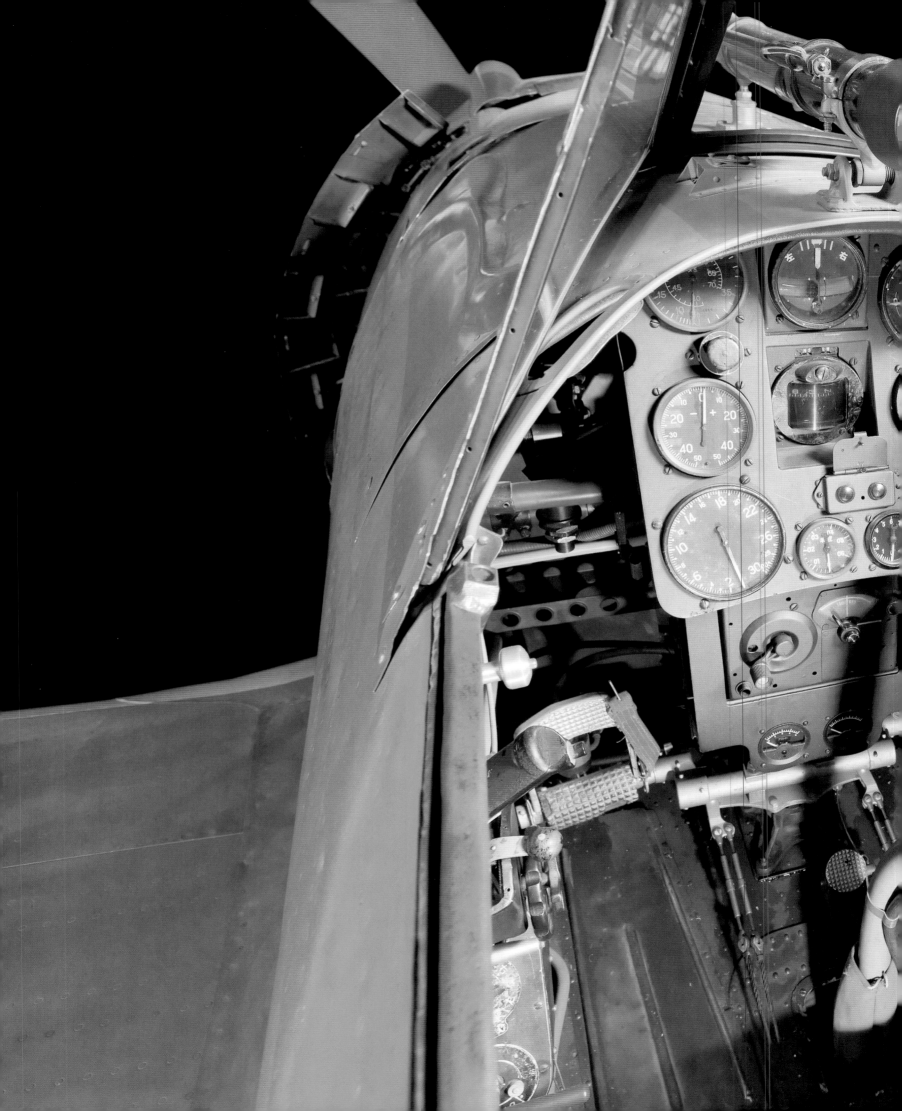

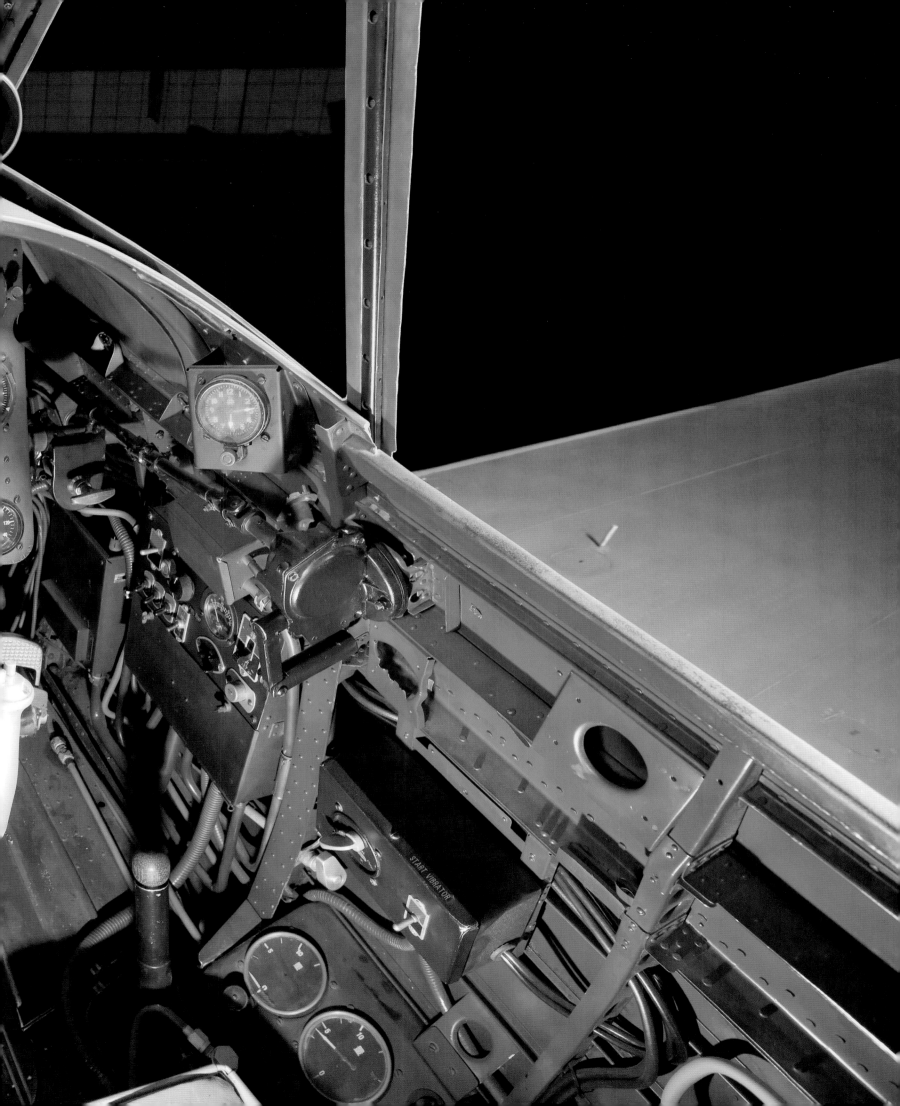

concealed in jungle and would be most difficult to detect from the air. There is only foot tracks leading to each aircraft and no roads to give their positions away. Besides this, each aircraft is covered in camouflage netting.

"I managed to find the Oscar hidden some distance from the strip again and found three men working on it. Vahry was able to get a photograph of it with the men."

The plan was to remove the airplane and fly the fighter to the airfield at Jacquinot Bay in New Britain. However, things didn't go as desired. Hamilton relates: "The Oscar has now been almost completely reassembled at the strip and looks as if it should be ready to fly in a couple of days. The Japanese have sent a message that it is not actually serviceable and we interviewed an engineer warrant officer out there. It is difficult to tell whether they actually are unable to repair it completely and I am inclined to think that they just don't want to fly it."

In any case, by December 1945, Hamilton got tired of waiting and had the plane crated and shipped to Australia. Under the jurisdiction of the War Department, the crate sat untouched for years. It was offered to the Australian War Memorial Museum in Canberra and accepted on July 14, 1949.

The Oscar was not considered as rare as it is today and the museum chose not to keep it, selling the plane to R. G. Curtis of Sydney in 1953. Curtis, in turn, sold it to Sid Marshall in 1962. The new owner stored the plane suspended in his hangar at Bakerstown Airport. Throughout the 1980s and 1990s the plane passed through many hands, ending up with Tim Wallis in 1994.

The plane had a lot of exterior damage—both from bullets and shrapnel, as well as scars from being carelessly transported over the years. As a complete restoration commenced, much more battle damage became apparent. Removing panels and skins, restorers found damage that had been quickly fixed in the field with lockwires and hasty patches.

Also apparent were the faint lightning bolt of the 11th Sentai on the tail and three chevrons over the rear of the fuselage. Interviews with JAAF personnel revealed that the red lightning flash on the tail signified the 11th Sentai's 2nd Squadron. The chevrons were faded so thoroughly that no one knew their real color. They were originally painted white during the restoration. Japanese veterans visiting the project told the restorers that the chevrons would have been yellow, and that the three stripes were carried on the plane assigned to the third flying position. The chevrons were painted yellow the following day.

By September 1995, the Ki-43 was pushed outside and filled with one hundred liters of fuel. On the second try, the Oscar's overhauled engine caught and fired, running for the first time in over fifty years.

The plane was taxied, but "not flown," for the public at the Warbirds Over Wanaka air show in 1996. Photographs of the event show the aircraft with its gear definitely off the grass by as much as three feet. The aircraft appeared at the premier New Zealand aircraft exhibition throughout the late 1990s. In December 1999, the Oscar was sold to the FHC.

It is one of the few aircraft at the FHC that does not fly regularly. Tim Wallis's wife, Prue Wallis, wrote: "Although operationally it would be quite possible to render the plane flyable, it is likely that the *Hayabusa* will never leave the ground again. The value of the aircraft far outweighs the gamble—to lose the Oscar through misadventure would be to lose an entirely unique part of Japanese and World War II history."

ABOVE: This image shows the FHC's Oscar during restoration. Workers carefully marked the locations of the plane's original insignia before removing the deteriorating paint. Note the rectangular bullet hole patches in the tail. They are still visible today.

PREVIOUS PAGES: The cockpit of the Oscar shows a blue green metallic paint, called *aotake*. The unusual color was added to the semi-transparent anti-corrosion covering to help assure that it was applied to every part of the plane's interior.

OPPOSITE: The Oscar's "butterfly flaps" helped generate lift and improved stability at low speeds by increasing the fighter's wing area, further tightening the Oscar's already tight turning radius. With these flaps deployed, there was no way a P-39 or P-40 flyer could compete with the Ki-43 in a turning duel.

The FHC's A6M3-22 Zero was all but destroyed on the ground at Babo airfield in New Guinea, most likely during an American air attack.

THE ICONS

MITSUBISHI A6M3-22 REISEN (ZERO)

NORTH AMERICAN P-51D MUSTANG

Some aircraft became the symbols of their nations during wartime, as was certainly the way with Great Britain's Supermarine Spitfire. On the other side of the world, a navy fighter aircraft became the prominent face of Japan's war effort—from the attack on Pearl Harbor to the final desperate days of the *kamikaze*.

The story of the Mitsubishi A6M Zero naval fighter parallels that of Nakajima's Oscar in many ways. However, the Zero was a more dominant weapon at the start of the fighting, it was somewhat more successfully upgraded than the Oscar, and the plane faded into obsolescence at a slower rate.

Both the Zero and Oscar followed in the footsteps of their fixed-gear older brothers. In the case of the Zero, it was the A5M carrier fighter designed by Mitsubishi. The Japanese Navy made their final specification for a new naval fighter in late 1937 based on combat reports coming back from the conflict in China. Among other requirements, the plane had to fly at over 311 mph, climb 9,840 feet in nine and a half minutes, cruise for up to eight hours with the use of drop tanks, carry two cannon and two machine guns, and be at least as maneuverable as the current frontline carrier fighter.

Mitsubishi's chief designer, Jiro Horikoshi, thought the task was nothing short of impossible. The aircraft that took shape over the months that followed was conventional in appearance and construction for the time, yet amazingly light. Designers adhered to an extremely strict weight-savings doctrine: They addressed and chopped weight on every part of the aircraft that was more than 1/100,000th of the final proposed weight

of the fighter. Little by little, Mitsubishi's designers found ways to shave precious kilograms, even grams, throughout the aircraft.

Other changes were more significant in making the plane nimble. The skin was made from a high-tech duralumin alloy—aluminum alloyed with copper, manganese, and magnesium. By comparison, an early Zero weighed 3,700 pounds empty while an American Grumman Wildcat carrier fighter from the same period weighed over 2,000 pounds more, tipping the scales at 5,895 pounds.

When it flew for the first time on April 1, 1939, the Zero met or surpassed most of the Japanese Navy's "impossible"

RIGHT: Japanese ace Hiroyoshi Nishizawa, photographed in his A6M3-22 Zero near the Solomon Islands in 1943. He had eighty-seven victories to his credit when he was killed. A Japanese cargo plane Nishizawa was riding in was shot down by American fighters.

ABOVE: Cowling off, the Zero is checked one last time before its "first flight" since restoration in Wenatchee, Washington. When the fighter took to the skies in 2012, it was the first time the Zero had flown in nearly seventy years.

OPPOSITE: Some Zero fighters were modified to carry an additional passenger. The FHC's aircraft is similar, with an elongated canopy to allow a second flyer to ride behind the pilot.

TOP: Moving back to front, painters look at their reference sheets to mimic the dark green stripes applied in the field. The paint goes on in chronological layers, with fresh coats sometimes obscuring intricate stencils that would have been applied at the Mitsubishi factory.

ABOVE: This close-up shows the two-piece cowling around the Zero's engine. Distinctive latch covers are held in place with Dzus fasteners that join the bottom and top sections of the engine covering.

requirements. "The trim wing cut sharply through the air and reflected the sunlight every time it turned over," Horikoshi later wrote. "I was almost screaming, 'It's beautiful,' forgetting for a moment, I was a designer."

At the outbreak of war with the United States, the Zero was the most potent carrier plane in the world. Speedy and agile, the Zero was the uncontested king of aerial combat in the Pacific for much of 1942. American pilots often had to work in pairs to defeat a single Zero in combat.

But like the Oscar, the Zero was fragile, with little in the way of protection in those early days. While Mitsubishi developed improved versions of the fighter, they were no match for bigger, more powerful aircraft like the F6F Hellcat and F4U Corsair. By mid war, the Zero was not only inferior to new American fighters, but the pool of skilled Japanese fighter pilots had shrunk considerably due to terrible losses.

The FHC's A6M3-22 Zero entered the war just as the tide began to turn against the Zero and the nation of Japan. The plane left Mitsubishi in the summer of 1943 and was most likely ferried into the New Guinea area through the Philippines. The hulk of the plane was found at Babo Airfield on Irian Jaya in what is now the Indonesian half of New Guinea. Through 1943 and the first half of 1944, the area had been exposed to many American bomber attacks and this plane was one of the unlucky aircraft that had been damaged by bombs.

Not only had the area seen violent attacks, but also it was later bypassed by the Allies, leaving many remarkably intact wrecks and abandoned Japanese airplanes. Babo was considered an almost mythical place in the eyes of aircraft salvagers by the 1970s and 1980s. A California aircraft salvager named Bruce Fenstermaker made a deal with local officials to obtain aircraft relics from the airfield in the early 1990s.

Fenstermaker's early actions in the area focused on an abandoned A6M3-22 Zero, which would become known as serial number 3869. After location and sale to the Santa Monica Museum of Flying (MOF), Fenstermaker and the MOF almost immediately agreed to participate in a joint venture to acquire more aircraft from the site before Indonesia withdrew permission, or other salvagers were able to mount efforts of their own.

By 1991, the group had acquired a Betty bomber, a Judy carrier plane, a Tony fighter, and parts of a Nick twin-engine fighter, and two other Zeros. The original Zero parts used in the rebuild of the FHC Zero reportedly came from this venture between the MOF and Fenstermaker.

ABOVE: The FHC's restoration and maintenance manager Jason Muszala guides the Zero under the photo plane in this dramatic shot. Note the bulges in front of the cockpit to accommodate the plane's pair of cowl-mounted Type 97 7.7mm machine guns.

ABOVE: The last version of the Zero made in large numbers was the A6M5-52. These planes are most recognizable by the series of exhaust stacks behind the engine cowling. This plane was captured by the US military and photographed during test flights.

BELOW: A blur of heat trails away from the Zero's radial engine. Originally built with a Nakajima Sakae 21, restorers chose to equip the FHC's example with a dependable R-1830. As a result, the plane has never missed a flying performance.

With a lack of basic building materials in the area, the salvagers paid natives to make crates from teak logs and branches tied together with hemp rope. One commentary on the project even suggests that the materials were obtained through the sale of some of the locals' homes, which were dismantled and reused as the unusual shipping "boxes." Efforts to get the three Zeros took "close to six years, covered two continents, and consumed in excess of 300,000 man-hours before all were actually restored to flying condition," according to Bruce Lockwood, then MOF Director of Restoration.

The three Zeros hulks, in varying degrees of disrepair, arrived in California in June 1991. After research, the planes were assigned serial numbers 3869, 3858, and 3852 (the FHC Aircraft). All were in very bad condition—with bomb damage, bullet holes, and years of corrosion from being exposed to the elements. As well, the skin and structure of each aircraft had been chopped away by the natives to make cooking utensils and weaponry.

The sheer volume of work finally led the MOF to make a deal with Flight Magic Inc. of Santa Monica to continue the

TIGER STRIPES

The FHC A6M3-22 Zero is a mid-war aircraft, so it doesn't fall cleanly into the category of either a sharp-looking Pearl Harbor-era Imperial Japanese Navy fighter, or an all dark-green A6M5s flying during the last phases of the conflict. Collection staffers began to think that they could use the Zero's paint scheme as a teaching tool, representative of Japan's fortunes in the Pacific at the time.

What is now on view is actually two schemes in one. These planes came from the factory looking one way and were quickly modified to meet the realities of operating from remote island outposts often under attack by marauding American aircraft.

Ryan Toews, of the website J-aircraft.com, sent the FHC a tiny fragment of original, painted aircraft skin, no bigger than a fingernail. This miniscule shard of aluminum helped staffers determine the precise light olive green color used by Mitsubishi when the planes were delivered from the factory in Japan. The olive color was sprayed on the aircraft to be followed by a multitude of factory-applied stencils and data blocks.

There were other details to the factory scheme. One included mixing in a dose of blue into the black cowling paint: Mitsubishi's black paint is reported to have had a slight blue tinge when viewed in the sunlight. Another had the FHC painters mimicking the color of the control surfaces, painted separately, by mixing a special batch of slightly lighter olive, masking off the rudder, ailerons, and flaps, and shooting them again.

After a few days, the plane looked like it had when it was delivered. It was now time to mottle it up a little bit. The olive-colored aircraft were too difficult to hide at their island bases. The planes stood out when observed from above and became easy targets. As a result, the order came down to cover the top surfaces with a dark shade of green.

Individual units in the field carried out the order in different ways, which made

for an interesting search to find the best scheme. FHC staffers started referring to the potential candidates by the characteristics of their camouflage—"turtle spots," "the giraffe," and "the zebra," among others. They settled on the one they called "tiger stripes."

The men of Air Group 251, based in the Rabaul area, chose to paint some of their planes in bold vertical stripes. The majority of the work on the restored plane was done by two different painters to replicate the look of the plane had it been shot by two mechanics hurriedly moving down their line of aircraft. It was slightly painful to hold the paint gun, pull the trigger, and shoot dark green paint over some the detailed stencils and artwork applied only days before, but it was all in the name of authenticity.

The Zero's distinctive tiger stripes were applied by Japanese mechanics in the field after the planes proved too easy to spot on the ground at their island air bases. The plane's unit markings were also partly obscured by the dark green paint.

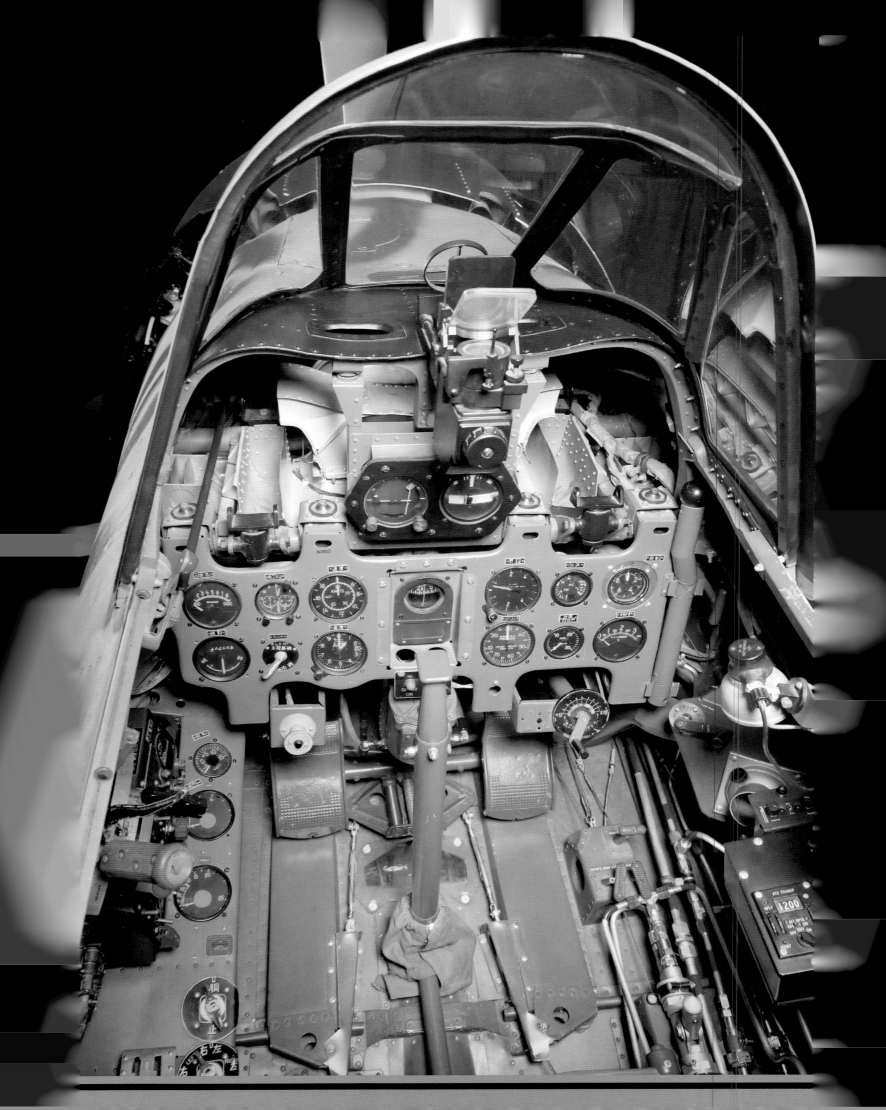

OPPOSITE: The Zero's cockpit is small but reasonably comfortable. Designers knew that A6M pilots would be flying up to eight hours over the vast reaches of the Pacific Ocean.

RIGHT: America unlocked the secrets of the vaunted Zero when one crash-landed during an attack in the Aleutian Islands. The plane was quickly rushed stateside for repair and technical evaluation.

BELOW: The Zero has small folding wingtips that allowed it to comfortably fit in the elevators of Japanese aircraft carriers. The raised tips reduced the span of the fighter by about four feet but kept the plane light and simple.

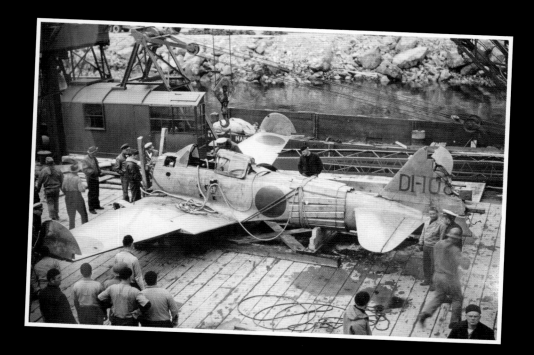

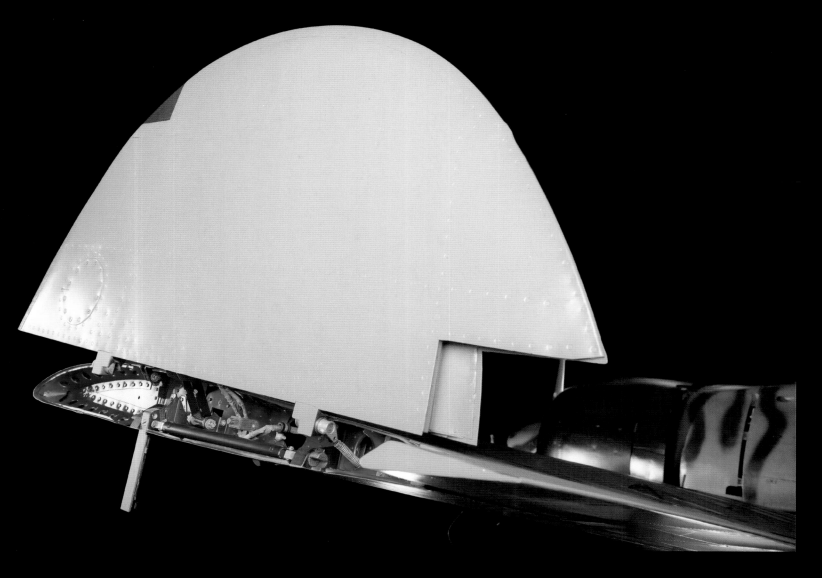

restorations more efficiently. This group had ties with an organization in Russia that had produced replica Yakovlev Yak-3 fighters powered with American Allison engines. The trio of Japanese fighters was transferred to Russia for completion in 1994. At almost the same time, the MOF unearthed a nearly complete set of Zero plans, which made a full restoration a much easier proposition.

Some original parts of each aircraft were used in the restorations, but since the planes were going to be flyable, "it would be mandatory that new materials and parts would have to be used in any area required to carry a structural load," explained Lockwood.

The rebuilt Zeros were sent back to California in 1997. American engines were judged much easier and cheaper to maintain than original Japanese Sakae powerplants, so each plane received a specially made Pratt & Whitney R-1830 engine. To keep them small enough to fit inside a Zero's cowling, each was made from an R-1830-75 power section, an R-1830-90 blower section, and an R-1830-94 accessory section—all mated together to work as a single unit.

The FHC aircraft was the last of the three to be completed. The first of the aircraft flew in California in 1998, the second

BELOW: A flight of four Mustangs prowl the skies over Italy, looking for targets. The planes each carry a pair of seventy-five-gallon external fuel tanks to extend their time in the air. When they see enemy aircraft, they can drop the tanks in order to be more nimble in a dogfight.

in 2000. This pair was shipped to Hawaii for the filming of the motion picture *Pearl Harbor*, which was released the following year.

The FHC purchased Zero 3852 in June 1998. This aircraft continued to be housed in Chino, California, at Fighter Rebuilders. Over time, the company worked to convert the plane to a two-seater—a feature seen with Zero aircraft used as wartime advanced trainers.

The Zero came to Washington in May 2008 and put on display for the opening of the FHC's Everett facility. In 2010, the Zero was dismantled and sent to Century Aviation in Wenatchee, Washington, for final preparations to return it to flying condition. On March 29, 2012 the plane made its maiden flight over Wenatchee with Steve Hinton as test pilot.

Today, the aircraft wears the paint scheme of a fighter from Kokutai (Air Group) 251, which served near Rabaul. The aircraft was factory-painted light olive and then painted over with dark green camouflage in the field.

The North American P-51 Mustang is arguably the greatest fighter of World War II. While some tout the Supermarine Spitfire as a better performer, historians point out that the Mustang's incredible range gave it an important edge. Mustangs could tangle with German fighters over Berlin or they could strafe an airfield near Tokyo, both too far from friendly airfields for the short-legged Spitfire.

The famous Mustang actually started life as a fighter for Great Britain. Well before Pearl Harbor, British Purchasing Committee officials approached California-based North American Aviation, Inc. (NAA), about building Curtiss P-40s under license for the RAF.

NAA's response was bold considering the fact that they had never made a high-performance fighter aircraft before. They said they could make a better plane than the P-40, and would design and build the first one in less than 120 days. Amazingly, NAA rolled the plane out the factory 117 days later—never mind the fact that it had borrowed wheels and no engine. Six weeks later, on October 29, 1940, the new plane flew for the first time with an Allison V-1710 engine.

The prototype Mustang, called the NA-73X, had an incredibly clean, yet simple, airframe. North American did away with many of the rounded shapes common to aircraft of the era, shapes that would take too long to tool and build. Instead, the plane had squared-off wings and tail surfaces.

ABOVE: The Mustang is considered one of the prettiest and most capable aircraft of World War II. Able to escort American bombers over long distances and take on the Luftwaffe's best aircraft, the P-51's war record was second to none.

The plane also flew with a distinctive cooling scoop designed with data acquired from Curtiss and NACA, and perfected by NAA engineers. The scoop contained the coolant radiator and supercharger aftercooler combined, as well as a separate cooler for oil.

Possibly the most impactful trait was the new fighter's laminar flow wing, also a result of NACA studies. The NACA number 66 airfoil was designed as symmetrically as possible by moving the thickest part of the wing aft. This allowed the air passing over the wing to maintain adhesion to the surface for as long as possible. It translated into less turbulence and drag on the wing, which led to a fighter that could fly faster and longer than the norm.

Great Britain, embroiled in fighting in Europe and North Africa, increased the order for what would be called the "Mustang," even before the first one flew. By contrast, the US Army was a bit more apprehensive about the aircraft before Pearl Harbor. To them, the Allison-powered Mustang looked no better than the Curtiss P-40. In addition, the army had no money for new fighter development.

NAA officials found that the army *did* have money for attack planes. The same aircraft, fitted with a dive brake and bomb

ABOVE: Right behind the Mustang's stick is the fuel tank selector switch. With it, the pilot can draw fuel from one of the fighter's internal tanks or external drop tanks. On more than one occasion during World War II, the switch broke off in a flyer's hand, leaving him with fuel, but no way to get to it. As a result, many Mustang pilots learned to carry a pair of pliers with them on long flights.

PREVIOUS PAGES: The FHC's North American P-51D Mustang is a combat veteran that served with the Eighth Air Force in England during World War II. The plane is one of only two Mustangs surviving today known to have shot down a German jet plane in combat.

racks, became the A-36 Apache. In April 1942 and now at war, the US Army ordered five hundred of them.

The A-36 and British Allison-powered Mustang were great planes below eighteen thousand feet, but quickly turned into a dog at higher altitudes. Both countries began working on the solution in 1942—crossing the excellent aerodynamic qualities of the Mustang with the performance of a Rolls-Royce Merlin engine. The British flew their version first, in October 1942.

Now the Mustang had it all. It could maneuver well, fly high, and cruise great distances. It could not have come at a better time for the Americans. US Army Air Forces officials had optimistically thought heavy bombers could defend themselves, but it was clear from nearly the beginning that daylight bombing raids over Germany and Occupied Europe would be incredibly costly. Escort planes like the Spitfire, P-47, and P-38 didn't have the fuel capacity to stay with the bombers over great distances, and, when the fighter escort departed, the Luftwaffe moved in for the kill.

The Mustang changed all that. This fighter could stay with the bombers during practically the whole flight and, when the enemy appeared, the P-51 could fight it out with the best of them.

After his capture, Luftwaffe chief Hermann Goering was asked when he knew the war was over. Goering replied, "When I saw your bombers over Berlin protected by your long-range fighters [Mustangs], I knew then that the Luftwaffe would be unable to stop your bombers. Our weapons plants would be destroyed; our defeat was inevitable."

The FHC's P-51D Mustang was built in the North American Inglewood, California, factory in January 1945. The army accepted the plane on January 22, 1945 and transported it overseas in February.

The plane joined the Eighth Air Force, 353rd Fighter Group, 352nd Fighter Squadron and was assigned to Lt. Harrison B. "Bud" Tordoff, who quickly christened it with the same name of his previous Mustang—*Upupa epops*. While flying P-47s, Tordoff had three confirmed air-to-air victories—all Bf 109s.

By the time his squadron had switched to Mustangs, there were strict rules for naming aircraft and each proposed name was approved by Eighth Air Force headquarters. A former ornithology (study of birds) student at Cornell University before enlisting, Tordoff "had been taken with the euphonious scientific name, *Upupa epops*," the Latin name of a robin-sized bird, the hoopoe, found in southern Europe and Asia, and parts of Africa.

This was an ironic name for the Mustang; an inside joke. Tordoff recalls textbooks citing the hoopoe as a bird with "a bizarre appearance," "weak flying ability," and "untidy nesting habits." The bureaucrats at Eighth Air Force headquarters, busy sorting out suggestive and inappropriate names, approved *Upupa epops* without even a hint of a challenge.

GUN CAMERA

ABOVE: Sometimes mistaken for a German Bf 109 by overanxious Allied pilots and gun crews, the P-51D Mustang's distinctive scoop and bubble canopy set it apart, should the attacker get more than a split second look at the plane.

PREVIOUS PAGES: The Mustang's Merlin engine is shoehorned into its streamlined nose. Built by Packard in the United States, the addition of the British-designed Merlin made the P-51 a world-beater.

Tordoff flew the original *Upupa epops* during his first tour, from October to December 1944, completing fifty-nine missions. Then Tordoff went home for a brief visit. Upon returning to his squadron in February 1945, he was assigned the FHC Mustang, serial number 44-72364.

Captain Tordoff flew 26 more combat missions in the second *Upupa epops* from March 1945 until VE-Day. On March 31, Tordoff's unit encountered several jet-powered Me 262s fighters while escorting B-17s to Derben. Only Tordoff scored, his plucky, and perhaps somewhat sarcastic, report read:

> I was leading Jockey Red flight on an escort mission to Derben, Germany. About 20 minutes before target time, several (perhaps 5 or 6) Me 262's [sic] appeared. The ones I saw were above me, so our squadron stayed with the bombers rather than give chase. Fifteen minutes later we were at 23,000 ft. on the right side of our combat group of bombers. I called out two bogies approaching us from 9 o'clock. Because I neglected to say also that they were low, about 16-17,000 ft, no one else saw them until they passed under us. I then identified them as Me 262's, so I told my flight to drop their tanks and bounce them. Although we had lost our chance for the most advantageous bounce by failing to recognize them until they had passed under us, I still had enough altitude to close on the rearmost

jet to about 700 yards. At this extreme range I opened fire and using my time-tested and battle-proven theories of aerial gunnery, I obtained my usual fine results—one strike on the left jet unit (and this only after firing 1,545 rounds) What appeared to be gas, started streaming out of the left jet, but he still pulled away from me. Being somewhat unhappy over this apparent waste of ammunition, I decided to follow him home to see if he might spin in in the traffic pattern or something. We chased the two of them for about eight minutes with everything wide open, but still fell behind. At last we came to an airdrome, and the 262's now about two miles ahead of us decided to split up. The one with both good jets made a diving turn to the left, and my numbers 3 and 4 followed him while the one I had hit pulled up into about a 60-degree climb, still streaming gas. I cut him off, thinking he was going to do an Immelmann, but instead, his jet very nicely burst into flame and out popped the pilot. The 262 then spun down burning and almost hit me. Recovering from the spin, it dove straight into the ground and exploded. I looked for the pilot, but unfortunately could not find him. As usual, I forgot to take any pictures of the plane while it was burning, but nevertheless, I claim one Me 262 destroyed—by one .50 cal bullet.

Tordoff's fifth official aerial victory, another Bf 109, came on April 17, 1945, while escorting bombers to Hamburg. Tordoff continued to fly the plane until he was shipped home in August 1945. His Mustang, however, stayed in Germany.

After a period of occupation, the United States began to get rid of much of their air arsenal in Europe. Some fighters and bombers were chopped apart for scrap. Others were ferried home. Still other aircraft were sold to countries clamoring for modern machines. Sweden acquired their first batch of forty-three Mustangs before the war in Europe had ended—for $160,000 apiece.

By March 1946, the purchase of a second batch of ninety ex-combat Mustangs was negotiated with the US military— Sweden paid $3,500 each for these aircraft. *Upupa epops* was one of this batch of ninety transferred from an airbase in Germany to Sweden in late 1946. Designated J 26 Mustangs, these planes served with Swedish Fighter Wing F 16 at Uppsala and F 4 at Ostersund.

By the early 1950s, Sweden was looking to acquire more modern jet aircraft and began to dispose of the Mustangs through sale. Mustangs were sold to Israel, the Dominican Republic, and Nicaragua, and the former *Upupa epops* was one of thirty-two Mustangs that went to the Dominican Republic in late 1952.

ABOVE: Ace pilot Harrison "Bud" Tordoff poses for a photograph with his plane, *Upupa epops*, in 1945. The distinctive yellow and black checkered field surrounding the noses of the planes of the 353rd Fighter Group Mustangs was enlarged during the conflict to allow for better visibility. Ground crews skipped the checkers that would have covered the plane's nickname nose art.

The *Fuerza Aerea Dominicana* (FAD) had acquired older versions of the Mustang, including some Allison-powered airplanes, as early as 1948. The FAD was not only the first Latin American air force to operate Mustangs, it was also the last to retire them from service.

The Dominican Republic's dictator, Rafael Trujillo, gathered as many fighting aircraft as he could to help weather invasion attempts from Cuba and Guatemala in the late 1940s. Tensions with Haiti, as well as the availability of Swedish Mustangs, led to the purchases in 1952 and later. The former *Upupa epops* was assigned the designator FAD 1916—part of a group of over forty fully operational Mustangs used by the Dominican Republic at the time.

By 1957, Trujillo's Mustang fleet was dwindling due to operational losses and accidents. Relations with the United States and many other countries were falling apart, making it difficult to get spare parts. The dictator wanted to sell nearly

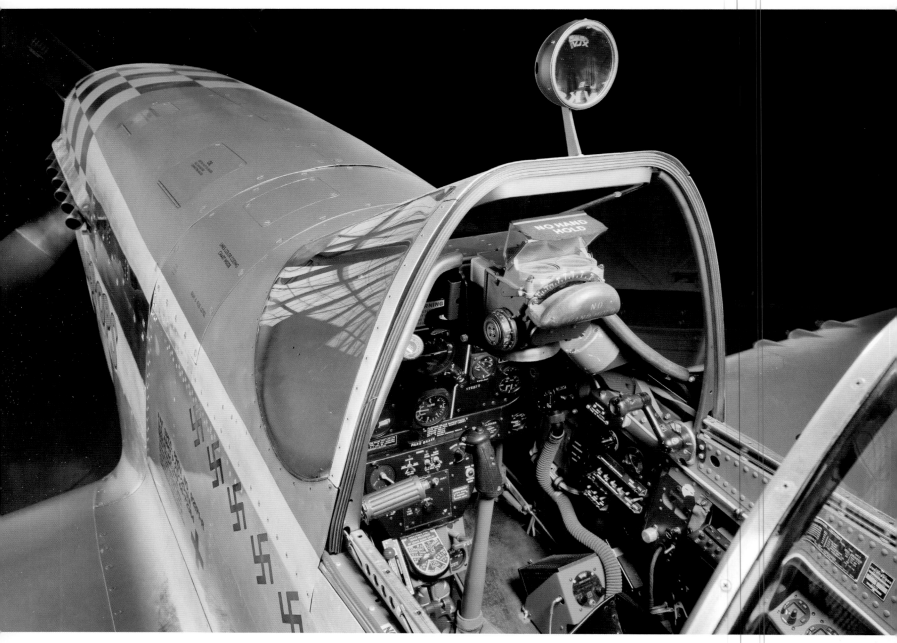

ABOVE: While most of the Mustang's fuselage is bare metal, the area in front of the cockpit is painted olive drab. The dull color assures that the pilot will not be blinded by sunlight reflecting off the top of the fighter's cowling. During World War II, this plane flew with one piece of non standard equipment—a mirror unit stolen from a downed Spitfire. Today, the mirror is still perched on top of the windscreen.

PREVIOUS PAGES: The North American P-51D was a fighter pilot's dream—powerful engine, great visibility, and six trusty .50-caliber guns. Considered by many to be the archetypical fighter of World War II, the plane fought again in Korea. The last example to serve in a US tactical unit was retired from the West Virginia Air National Guard in 1957.

all the Mustangs in favor of jet fighters, but could not strike a deal. Invasion attempts kept coming through the late 1950s and the FAD Mustangs were used to counter each new threat. Dominican Mustangs even had a pair of run-ins with US Navy aircraft. It is quite likely that the FHC Mustang was used in combat at some point during its time in Latin America.

FAD continued to shrink after Trujillo was assassinated in 1961. Unable to acquire "better" aircraft, the Dominican Republic used a company in Florida to overhaul the fighters in 1965. Tran-Florida Aviation Inc., predecessor to Cavalier Aircraft Corporation, worked on about thirty-six of the remaining Mustangs with US State Department approval.

During the civil war of 1965, the FAD Mustangs and some P-47s were again used in combat. When US Marines were sent to the country as peacekeepers, they too were involved in combat with the Mustangs—one FAD F-51 mistakenly attacked marine ground forces and another was shot down by US ground fire when it strafed near the US embassy. By 1968, FAD reportedly had about twenty-four Mustangs undergoing a second major overhaul.

Amazingly, the Mustangs were used by the Dominican Republic until 1984—the last known Mustangs in armed service for a nation. That year, the Dominican Republic replaced the ancient fighters with ex-USAF Cessna OA-37B Dragonfly attack planes. Depending on the source, eight to twelve of the original Mustangs, including FAD 1916, remained.

The future FHC plane was slated to become a gate guard display aircraft at San Isidro air base, but the sale price of these remaining aircraft, reportedly $300,000 each, convinced someone in the FAD to let the plane go to a private buyer in the United States.

Called the "last bulk warbird sale" by *Air & Space Magazine*, nine Mustangs and masses of spare parts were purchased by Brian O'Farrell and Johnson Aviation of Miami, Florida, in 1984. FAD 1916 was the only aircraft of the group not purchased by private investors in the late 1980s. In early 1998, the FHC acquired this last Mustang from Brian O'Farrell.

The plane was sent to WestPac Restorations Inc. in Rialto, California. There, the Mustang underwent a restoration process of unprecedented detail and accuracy, creating one of the most complete P-51 Mustangs in the world. In the words of WestPac President Bill Klaers, "[I]t was agreed that this aircraft would not only be restored, but that it would also be returned to exactly the same standard as it was in when it left the North American Aviation factory in late 1944."

RIGHT: One pair of the P-51D Mustang's guns is staggered aft. Early versions of the fighter only had four .50-calibers and when North American designers added another pair, there was no place for the ammunition boxes and feed shoots within the wing. The solution was to back up the new set of guns by a few inches—about the length of a .50-caliber bullet—and build in another set of ammo boxes behind the originals.

In the summer of 2003, Bud Tordoff, now living in Minnesota, came to Arlington, Washington and was reunited with his aircraft. It was the first time he'd seen it since the end of the war. He wrote in the right gun bay door of the fighter, "I flew this plane in combat, March and April of 1945. It always brought me home."

Tordoff was able to come back to see "his" Mustang after it had had been moved to the new FHC museum facility at Paine Field for the June 6, 2008 opening. Soon after, on July 23, 2008, Harrison "Bud" Tordoff passed away.

ABOVE: When pilots talk about flying, they can't help but use their hands. Here, a pair of flyers from the 350th Fighter Squadron relive a story of air combat over Occupied Europe.

The FHC's Focke-Wulf Fw 190 A-5 was lost in combat over Russia and located, undisturbed, decades later. It is today the only flying Fw 190 in the world.

THE
BUTCHER
BIRDS

FOCKE-WULF FW 190 A-5

FOCKE-WULF FW 190 D-13

The Focke-Wulf Fw 190's nickname, "Butcher Bird", is an Anglicized name within a nickname. The German slang term for the plane was "*Würger*," or shrike in English. The Germans were quite fond of unofficial bird names for their planes, like *Schwalbe* (swallow) for the Messerschmitt Me 262 jet plane and *Uhu* (owl) for the Focke-Wulf Fw 189 reconnaissance plane

Quoting a popular internet source on the bird, "Shrikes (the birds) are known for their habit of catching insects and small vertebrates and impaling their bodies on thorns. This helps them to tear the flesh into smaller, more conveniently sized fragments, and serves as a cache so that the shrike can return to the uneaten portions at a later time. This same behavior of impaling insects serves as an adaptation to eating the toxic lubber grasshopper. The bird waits for 1 to 2 days for the toxins within the grasshopper to degrade, and then can eat it."

So, the vicious shrike got the nickname "Butcher Bird," which, in some ways, is appropriate to the plane too. The Americans feared the Focke-Wulf Fw 190 because it was used to hound their bomber formations over Europe, constantly picking at the big group of bombers and then pouncing on any one that dropped out of formation. Their brutal

ABOVE: When this photo was taken, no one had flown a Focke-Wulf Fw 190 in nearly a half century. During this first flight, test pilot Steve Hinton explores the handling characteristics of the plane during modest maneuvers. Early flight calculations often also include learning the plane's stall speed.

tactics made the name for the Fw 190 seem more than fitting, "Shrikes are known for their habit of catching insects and small vertebrates and impaling their bodies on thorns. This helps them to tear the flesh into smaller, more conveniently-sized fragments, and serves as a cache so that the shrike can return to the uneaten portions at a later time. This same behavior of impaling insects serves as an adaptation to eating the toxic lubber grasshopper. The bird waits for one to two days for the toxins within the grasshopper to degrade, and then can eat it."

So, the vicious shrike got the nickname "Butcher Bird," which, in some ways, is appropriate for the plane too. The Americans feared the Fw 190 because it was used to hound their bomber formations over Europe, constantly harassing the big group of bombers and then pouncing on any aircraft that dropped out of formation. These brutal tactics made the name for the Fw 190 seem more than fitting.

Zero and Oscar . . . Spitfire and Hurricane . . . Mustang and Thunderbolt . . . With the creation of the Focke-Wulf Fw 190, Germany had found the counterpart to the Messerschmitt Bf 109. Initiated in 1937 as a back-up plan to the Messerschmitt, talented Focke-Wulf designers proposed two aircraft to the German Air Ministry, the first powered by a liquid-cooled Daimler-Benz and the second with an air-cooled BMW radial.

The radial seemed out of the question to the engineers at Focke-Wulf. A big, drag-inducing engine seemed like no way to power a frontline fighter airplane. Lead designer Kurt Tank and the others were shocked when they got to word to proceed with the BMW radial. This was in part, because Daimler-Benz V-12s were urgently needed for Bf 109s.

Tank went ahead, fitting the BMW 139 radial with a fan to move more air into the very tight-fitting cowling. The airframe was designed to be sturdy and yet simple enough to allow widespread manufacture at many sub-manufacturing plants. The Fw 190 did away with one of the Bf 109's most frustrating weaknesses by featuring a wide-track landing gear that made it easier to handle on the ground.

Test pilots were impressed when the Fw 190 flew for the first time on June 1, 1939. The new plane was balanced, responsive, and fast. Another experimental version of the plane had a newly designed BMW 801 engine, which was more powerful and heavier, but roughly the same size as the 139. Once it was

proven, designers decided the 801 engine would be best for the new fighter.

The new 801 came with another pioneering piece of aviation technology. An electro-mechanical computer handled all of the engine management systems for the pilot. A flyer need only move the throttle and the *Kommandogerät* computed and set the proper fuel mixture, propeller blade pitch, boost, and timing.

The heavier 801 engine required a strengthening of the airframe and a readjustment of the plane's center of gravity. Pilots, who had been getting their feet roasted by the hot radial in flight, were quite pleased when they learned that the cockpit would be moved aft on production versions of the 190.

When it reached combat in the summer of 1941, the Fw 190 was a shock to British pilots flying their Spitfire V aircraft. The 190 could roll better, climb quicker, and dive steadier than the

BELOW: This image shows one the FHC's Focke-Wulf's "sister aircraft" during operations in Russia. White aircraft identification *letters*, as opposed to numbers, was a bit of an oddity for JG 54. The FHC's aircraft was "White A."

LEFT: Though it is often removed before a flight, the FHC has the original BMW logo plate for the plane's 801 engine. The artwork, familiar to most today, represents a propeller spinning in the blue Bavarian sky.

BELOW: Early one morning, when the desert air is cool and calm, restorers fire up the rare Focke-Wulf fighter to conduct taxi tests. Before ever getting into the air, flyers work with the plane as much as they can on the ground in an effort to learn everything they can about the fighter's brakes, instruments, controls, and steering ability before getting airborne.

PREVIOUS PAGES: This view of the 190's belly reveals the ammunition compartments for the plane's pair of wing-mounted MG 151 20mm cannon. The paint behind the cowling discolored from exposure to the BMW engine's hot exhaust gases.

ABOVE: During test flights in Arizona, the FHC's Fw 190 A-5 is photographed just inches from touchdown. Pilot Steve Hinton takes one last look over the nose of the plane's big BMW 801 engine before the fighter settles onto its tail wheel.

RAF fighters. And, if the combat situation favored the Spitfires, the 190's superior speed allowed German pilots to simply pull away from the threat. It was not until the arrival of the next generation Spitfire, the Mark IX, that the RAF regained superiority over the English Channel.

The Fw 190, with heavy firepower and the ability to fly to 37,000 feet was a brutal foe of American heavy bombers. However, Focke-Wulf fighters did not perform as well as the Messerschmitt fighters at altitudes above 21,000 feet. The 190 A-model shined at lower levels.

Soon, Focke-Wulf started modifying, then building ground-attack versions of the sturdy, dependable aircraft. The Germans called them *Jabos*—short for *Jagdbomber*, pursuit bomber or fighter bomber. The FHC aircraft was a Focke-Wulf Fw 190 A-5 modified for *Jabo* work. The plane carried more armor than fighter versions, and had a pair of cannon removed from the wings to allow more lifting capacity for bombs.

ABOVE: The FHC's Focke-Wulf fighter was found in such a remote location that it had to be lifted from its swampy environs by helicopter. The plane was transported to solid ground where crews could use heavy tools and equipment to carefully dismantle the plane for transport.

The FHC's aircraft was built in April 1943 as part of a batch of 981 aircraft at the Focke-Wulf factory in Bremen. Soon after, it was flown to the Eastern Front in May 1943. The plane was assigned to 4./JG 54—*Jagdgeschwader* 54, *Staffel* 4—at Siverskiy, south-southwest of Leningrad, in June or early July.

JG 54 had flown in support of the attack on northern Russia starting in the summer of 1941. Now, in the summer of 1943, the Russians had broken the siege of Leningrad by opening a narrow swath of land—called the "Corridor of Death"—just

OPPOSITE: The Fw 190's bucket seat has room for a "seat pack" parachute for the flyer. To the left of the gunsight are the plane's modern radios, which are used to communicate with Paine Field's tower during Fly Days.

PREVIOUS PAGES: To keep the nose around the fighter's engine as small and streamlined as possible, the Fw 190 A has a unique oil cooler located behind an armored cowling ring at the front of the plane. The delicate circle-shaped radiator took months to build and was particularly troublesome during the plane's first year flying with the FHC.

south of Lake Ladoga, and 4./JG 54 was tasked with flying interdiction missions against supply trains.

Feldwebel Paul Ratz was flying the FHC aircraft on the day it was lost. Ratz was a veteran of 117 combat missions and had shot down three Russian aircraft. On July 19, 1943 Ratz and his wingman were on a "free hunt" mission over the Corridor of Death looking for trains. Near Voybokalo the pair encountered heavy antiaircraft fire from a train and Ratz reported engine trouble. Ratz was listed as missing in action and, in fact, spent years as a POW in Russia.

The FHC's aircraft lay virtually untouched in a muddy forest for over forty-five years. Ratz's flying helmet was found placed neatly on the pilot's seat.

Rupert Wilbraham of the Soviet British Creative Association spearheaded the discovery of wrecks in the Russian wilderness. His group received a remarkable video tape of the Fw 190, hidden in a forest.

Ratz piloted his powerless Fw 190 to a nearly perfect belly landing in a swampy area covered with small saplings. Over time, the growing trees concealed the aircraft. It took a Soviet

RIGHT: During an FHC Fly Day performance, Germany's deadly duo perform for the crowds. Luftwaffe Day is one of the most popular flying exhibitions at the Flying Heritage Collection. Note the stream of "drool" from the Focke-Wulf's cowling-mounted oil cooler.

helicopter to lift the plane to a nearby town where it was disassembled and shipped to the United Kingdom.

Soon after, Doug Arnold of Warbirds of Great Britain Ltd. acquired the aircraft. Arnold's family eventually sold the aircraft to the FHC in 2001.

The major focus of restoration in the early years was the wing. Arthur Bentley, a former British Aerospace engineer, was instrumental in designing the wing jig. By August 1998, Jeremy Moore Engineering was involved in the next stage of restoration—the fuselage and engine cowling. The restorers found a number of field repairs and heavy wear, all indicating that the plane was in heavy use during its short operational life.

It was readily apparent at the time of recovery that Ratz and his Fw 190 were not downed by antiaircraft fire; there was no damage from enemy bullets. The engine had, in fact, overheated and seized. Sabotage is alleged and the date "5.7.43," fourteen days before the crash, was painted on the front of the

newly overhauled BMW engine. German maintenance facilities often used slave labor to rebuild engines.

Decades later, the BMW engine was rebuilt at Vintage V-12s in Tehachapi, California. The plane was imported into the United States in September 2006 and underwent final restoration at GossHawk Unlimited in Arizona. In early 2011, the plane was test flown for the first time by Steve Hinton. This rare fighter is the only flying example of the Fw 190 left in the world today.

However, the Fw 190 A-5 is not the only Focke-Wulf fighter at the FHC. The amazing collection also holds an equally rare example of a late-war "long-nosed" version of the famous Butcher Bird.

The Fw 190 A-model's drop in performance as it climbed over 21,000 feet was a hindrance for the Luftwaffe. The last years of fighting saw hundreds, then thousands of American high-flying heavy bombers over Germany. The D-model version of the Focke-Wulf 190 was designed to rectify the deficiencies at high altitude.

AS GERMANY FALLS

A side-by-side comparison of the FHC's two Focke-Wulf Fw 190 aircraft reveals a little about how the war was going for Germany in that final year. The Focke-Wulf Fw 190 A-5 aircraft, built in 1943, is an engineering marvel. The workmanship is complex, high quality, and always functional. As one restorer told the writer, "If the job could be done with fifty parts, the Germans chose to do it with a thousand."

By the time the scattered parts of the Fw 190 D-model aircraft were joined for final assembly, sacrifices had to be made to get planes into service as quickly as possible. With supplies of metals dwindling, aircraft manufacturers looked to use what was available. Whereas the early model Focke-Wulf is all metal, the D-model Focke-Wulf has flaps and propeller blades fashioned from wood.

In the paint shop, the earlier Fw 190 received intricate national insignia and a multitude of functional stencils on the landing gear legs, ammunition doors, and so on. The painters of the Dora did away with most of the placards in order to speed up the process. The swastika on the A-model 190 is a complex pattern of black with a white background and a black outline at its edges. On the D-model 190, overworked painters simply applied the symbol in black.

The final example, though small, perhaps best tells the story of Germany's collapse. On the top of the plane there

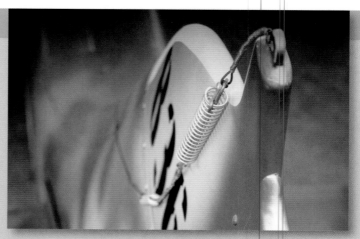

ABOVE: The Focke-Wulf Fw 190 D-13's antenna wire droops against the fuselage when the canopy is open. Earlier versions of the fighter had a reel to take up the slack when needed, but by the time late-model Luftwaffe fighters came from the factories, designers and workers had to cut corners to get the planes in combat quickly.

is an antenna wire that runs from the canopy to the tail. On the early model fighter there is a compact and complex aerodynamically faired, spring-loaded pulley that takes up the slack in the wire as a pilot slides the canopy backward. Rushed builders had come up with a different solution to the canopy retraction issue by the time the Fw 190 D came out of the factory. They said, "To heck with it . . ." When the canopy is open on the D-model, the wire simply droops onto the plane's fuselage.

The key to a newer, better version of the Focke-Wulf centered on its engine. The BMW 801 engine powering the Fw 190 A-model, even supercharged or turbocharged, could only generate so much horsepower.

By 1944, Kurt Tank had fitted a new Junkers Jumo 213A-1 powerplant into a Focke-Wulf airframe. The long, liquid-cooled, supercharged V-12 engine generated 2,240 horsepower; by comparison, the BMW 801 D-2 used in many early 190s topped out at about 1,670 horsepower.

It was a real engineering feat to install a Jumo 213 engine in a plane built to fly with a radial engine. The big Jumo pulled the Focke-Wulf's center of gravity forward dramatically. In order to balance the airframe quickly, designers created a fifty-centimeter "plug" to elongate the rear of the fuselage.

The longer fighter, with its enlarged tail planes and distinctive, annular radiator, looked quite different from earlier 190s. The D-model Focke-Wulf was often called "Dora" by German flyers; American fighter pilots simply called them "long-nosed" Focke-Wulfs.

At first Luftwaffe aviators were suspicious of this mutated version of their beloved fighter. They were won over once they saw the Fw 190 D in the air. The D-model could climb, turn, and maneuver well, even at great heights. The plane was faster than earlier models, too. The D-model was decidedly the best version of the 190.

The aircraft was great, but the outlook for Germany was brutally bleak by the time D-model fighters went into service. Though it was one of the most advanced piston-engine aircraft of its time, lack of fuel, threatened production facilities, and a

BELOW: The FHC's 190 D is the last example of its kind in the world—one of the very few aircraft in the collection that does not fly. However, periodically, when staffers are moving aircraft on a sunny day, the rare plane is moved outside for temporary display.

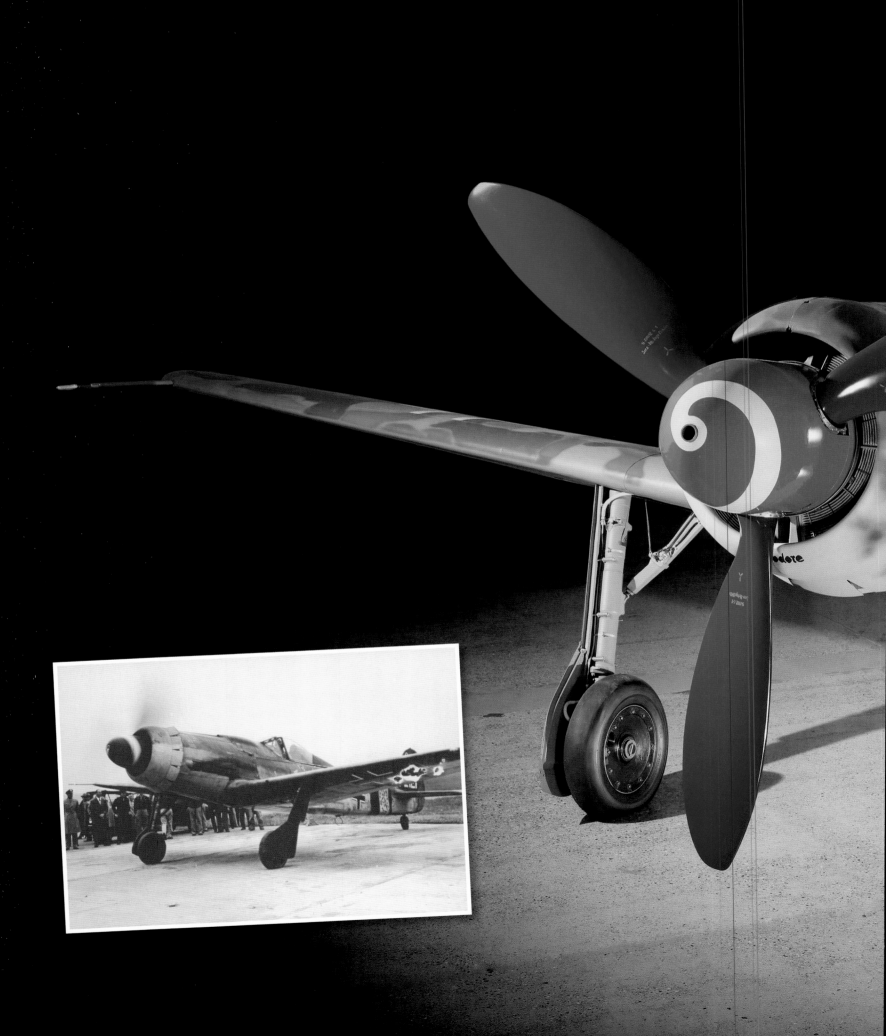

PREVIOUS PAGES: The FHC's Focke-Wulf Fw 190 D-13 was flown in combat until the end of World War II. Turned over to the Allies, it is the only D-13 model Focke-Wulf left in the world today. INSET: Officials stand by as a Focke-Wulf Fw 190 D-9 is readied for flight. The D-9 version was the most plentiful example of the D-model aircraft and is distinguishable from the FHC's D-13 by the pair of 13mm MG 131 machine guns in its nose, necessitating a bulged upper faring forward of the cockpit.

BELOW: If you hang upside down and crawl between the rudder pedals of the Fw 190 D-13, you can catch a glimpse of the butt of the plane's third MG 151 20mm cannon. Earlier attempts by German designers to make centerline guns had met with mixed results. Pilots complained of excessive noise, heat, and vibration. By the time the D-model came around, the gun worked at an acceptable level.

LEFT: Evidence of German's struggles with materials as their sphere of influence shrank can be seen in many parts of the late war Fw 190 D-13. Here, we see the plane's flaps, made from plywood instead of the aluminum used in earlier model Focke-Wulf aircraft.

grim shortage of skilled, veteran pilots rendered this potent aerial weapon nearly worthless.

Components of the FHC's Fw 190 D-13 were created at many different factories in Germany during that last desperate year of World War II—wings at Bernburg, fuselage at Nordenham, tail section from Leipzig, and various fuselage and wing components from Halle. The parts were most likely brought together at an *Arbeitsgruppe Roland* factory, possibly at Mimetall-Erfurt.

After construction, the aircraft was assigned to the Luftwaffe's *Jagdgeschwader* 26, which was based in northwestern Germany. "Yellow Ten" became the mount of the *Geschwader Kommodore* (wing commander) of JG 26, Maj. Franz Götz. Though now the leader of JG 26, Götz had spent much of his combat time in JG 53 where he racked up an impressive tally of victories against Allied aircraft. Götz's aircraft carried the ace of spades insignia, called the "*Pic As*" emblem, of the flyer's former unit, JG 53. The aircraft also had the word "*Kommodore*" under the lower radiator cowl to identify the leader's aircraft.

Götz was credited with sixty-three victories, including three heavy bombers, by the end of World War II. Franz Götz reportedly delivered the Fw 190 D-13 to an RAF unit then based near Flensburg at the end of the fighting. The plane was destined for evaluation in the United States, so small white stars were hastily painted on the wings and fuselage along with the designator: "USA 14." Later still, the D-13 would receive a second Allied designator—FE-118. The "FE" stood for Foreign Equipment.

Nearby British flyers became quite interested in the plane while it was at Flensburg and asked German pilots to fly the D-13 in mock combat with a Hawker Tempest. On at least two such occasions the German fighter, stripped of ammunition and carrying very little fuel, carried out faux dogfights with lightly-loaded Hawker aircraft. The fights between these two advanced piston-engine aircraft were often considered a draw—solely dependent on the skills of the pilots versus the qualities of the aircraft.

From Flensburg, the D-13 was ferried to an airbase in Holland and then to the port of Cherbourg, France. By July 19,

ABOVE: A single wing-mounted 20mm cannon passes through the landing gear bay and spar in each wing of the D-13. The scoop seen on the fuselage is used to feed air to the plane's side-mounted supercharger. When the fighter was owned by Bud Weaver and was parked outside, the scoop was torn off by "some rampaging drunk," wrote restorers. It took years to find the proper replacement.

Fw 190 (D.B. 603)

1945 the D-13 and forty other aircraft were loaded aboard the British escort carrier HMS *Reaper* for transport to the United States.

These aircraft were acquired by former US Army test pilot Col. Harold Watson and "Watson's Whizzers" as part of Operation Lusty—a mission to gain access to enemy aircraft, technical and scientific reports, research facilities, and weapons. The aircraft onboard the *Reaper* included ten Me 262s; five Fw 190 Fs; four Fw 190 Ds; one Ta 152 H; four Ar 234 Bs; three He 219s; three Bf 109s; two Do 335s; two Bu 181s; one WNF 342 helicopter; two Fl 282 helicopters; one Ju 88 G; one Ju 388; one Bf 108; and one US P-51 modified for reconnaissance. The planes were "cocooned" on the deck and crossed the Atlantic in the company of a group of intelligence researchers. Interestingly, the FHC's Messerschmitt Me 262 was another aircraft among this "deckload" that was brought to the United States in 1945.

At a port near Newark, New Jersey, the aircraft were divided. Some went to the navy, while others were bound for the army's Wright Field in Ohio. Still others, under the army's jurisdiction, were diverted to Freeman Field in Indiana when Wright Field could no longer handle additional aircraft. The D-13 was sent to Indiana. Among the 16,280 items and 6,200 tons sent for evaluation, the wings of the D-13 got mixed with those of a Focke-Wulf Fw 190 D-9 aircraft.

The D-13 fuselage and the D-9 wings were packed up and moved, along with an example of a Bf 109 G fighter, to be part of a static display at an airshow at Dobbins Air Force base near Marietta, Georgia. It is unknown whether the mechanics knew, or even cared, that the 190's wings were switched with another aircraft. The display was, of course, static, and the parts fit together well enough for public viewing.

Interest in propeller-driven aircraft waned as it became clear that jets would be the future of US military aviation. The authorities at Freeman Field did not want the German planes back at the end of the display period, so they were scheduled to be scrapped.

Circa 1946, the display aircraft were offered to Professor Donnell Dutton of the Georgia Institute of Technology in Atlanta. Dutton was the director of the Guggenheim School of Aeronautics at Georgia Tech and also was a member of the school's flying club. He accepted the planes and the D-13 was stored in a Navy hangar in Marietta, Georgia. It was there that it was discovered that the plane's engine-mounted MG 151 20mm cannon was still intact and loaded with ammunition.

The son of a former Georgia Tech student related that his father reported that the plane was running in roughly the 1946 to 1948 period, but it was missing its *Kommandogerät*, the engine management

ABOVE: The FHC's Focke-Wulf Fw 190 D-13 is beautifully restored inside and out. The padded leather sill carries the plane's Revi 16 reflector gunsight at the front of the cramped cockpit.

PREVIOUS PAGES: The Focke-Wulf Fw 190 D-13 represents the pinnacle of piston-powered aircraft. Along with the Super Corsair, Bearcat, Hawker Tempest, and a few others, the long-nosed 190 is among the last high-performance fighters built before the rise of the jet plane. INSET: A US Army artist created this drawing from descriptions of "long-nosed" Focke-Wulf fighters seen as the Allies forced their way across Occupied Europe. Most D-model 190s flew with Jumo 213 engines, though this illustration names the plane's engine as a DB 603.

computer. Engine speeds beyond idle were impossible without this "brain box." The student and others worked to create a new computer for the aircraft, but were not successful.

By the mid-1950s, both the Bf 109 and the Fw 190 were wrecks, having been vandalized and damaged. An FAA inspector named Bud Weaver traded an Aeronca Champ motor to the school for the two nearly priceless fighters. However, Weaver did not treat his new aircraft like valued relics; he moved them to various vacant lots and rental properties where they were even more damaged by collectors, curious teens, and vandals.

After Weaver passed away, his widow sold the hulk of the D-13 to an airline pilot, Lloyd Freeman. One of the first things Freeman did to the 190 was to strip off all of its original paint, which was, by then, faded and peeling. The unpainted plane was covered in a coat of zinc chromate. After this and a few other very minor improvements to the plane, he advertised it in an aviation trade publication.

Freeman sold the aircraft to Dave Kate of Santa Barbara, California. Kate wanted to restore the aircraft, but lacked the funds to get the job done. It is rumored that Kate and his associates may have been the first, since the D-13/D-9 wing switch, to note that the D-13 armament would not fit in the D-9 wings. This fact would be re-discovered by other restorers in the future.

The next buyer had both the desire and resources to see the rare aircraft restored to its wartime condition. Oklahoma oilman Doug Champlin acquired the Fw 190 in 1972 and had it shipped to Enid, Oklahoma. Soon, he struck a deal with Art Williams, an aircraft builder and restorer. The plane would be taken to Germany where it would be restored near Augsburg over a period of roughly two and a half years. Art's wife, Christina, was then working in the German aerospace field and could make contacts easily with those who had the unique skills to work on the airplane.

Interestingly, Focke-Wulf designer Kurt Tank assisted in the restoration by supplying wartime data and original manuals to the restorers. Of the many missing parts on the plane, the most troublesome were the "brain-box" controller and original propeller and hub. A D-9 spinner was used in the place of the original and a propeller was specially-crafted in Germany.

Again, the wings were discovered to be incorrect: "the ammo chutes . . . didn't line up with the armament, and no one could ever quite manage to get the ailerons connected to the control stick in a logical way." Data plates found inside the plane showed that the D-9 wings belonged to an aircraft held

ABOVE: The white stripe around the tail of the D-13 coincides with the plug installed in the tail to lengthen the plane's fuselage. The added length helps account for the longer Jumo 213 engine, shifting the center of gravity aft to compensate for the bigger power plant.

by the National Air and Space Museum but on display at the US Air Force Museum in Dayton, Ohio. That plane, in turn, was equipped with the D-13's wings.

Unable to convince officials at those institutions to make a trade, Champlin had the restored 190 shipped back to the United States in 1976. The plane was put on display with Champlin's extensive collection of other World War I and II fighter aircraft at a museum in Mesa, Arizona.

In 2001, GossHawk Unlimited started a second and more accurate restoration of the aircraft that involved undoing much of what had been done in the 1970s. This time, the wings were successfully traded for those on the D-9 and, after almost sixty years, the original wings were reunited with the D-13. During this restoration, all the original instrumentation, radios, and radio racks were placed back in the aircraft. The paint scheme was deduced from black-and-white photos of the original airplane and the colors matched to original factory paint chips.

While the 190 was in restoration, the rest of the Champlin collection was acquired by The Museum of Flight in Seattle. The high value of the Fw 190 D-13 precluded it from being part of a purchase funded by a Museum of Flight donor. So, the 190 was separated from the rest of Champlin's fighter collection.

When the D-13's restoration was finally completed in October 2004, Champlin chose to loan the plane to The Museum of Flight while looking for a buyer. In March 2007, the FHC purchased the aircraft from Champlin. Due to its extremely rare nature and high value, the fighter may never be flown.

The Fieseler Fi 156 C-2 *Storch* is one of the oddest-looking aircraft in the FHC's collection. Made to fly "slow and low" the plane is a far cry from the streamlined designs of planes like the Spitfire and Mustang.

ON THE ATTACK

7

FIESELER FI 156 C-2 *STORCH*

ILYUSHIN IL-2M3 *SHTURMOVIK*

NORTH AMERICAN B-25J MITCHELL

Pilots of pursuit aircraft, an early name for fighters, were often focused primarily on the war in the air. Interceptors and escorts usually worked to protect, or destroy, other aircraft. However, as many infantrymen are fond of saying, the important battles almost always take place on the ground.

Other types of aircraft were built to help, or harm, those struggling in that brutal world below the clear blue skies. The FHC aircraft described in this chapter had a significant impact on the battles on the ground. Several of the iconic aircraft in the collection excelled at aerial tasks, such as scouting, bombing, or ground attack.

The Fieseler Fi 156 C-2 was the antithesis of a sleek speedster like the Spitfire. No designer at the *Fieseler Flugzeugbau* cared at all about high speeds or firepower because the *Storch* was built to fly slow and low, taking on the duties of a liaison and observation aircraft.

There was nothing revolutionary about the plane's construction as the prototype took shape in 1935 and 1936. The fuselage of the aircraft was welded steel tubing, the wings were wood, and the entire exterior of the aircraft was covered in fabric. With no need to make the plane quick, a web of struts and bracing tubes surrounded the airframe. The gangly fixed landing gear hung down with a pair of too-small-looking tires attached. In the air, the plane

ABOVE: The *Storch* has "transit panels" on its wings and fuselage. The yellow areas were painted on German planes on the Eastern Front to keep German soldiers in Russia from firing at "friendly" aircraft.

resembled a stork getting ready to land on a rooftop; only those who flew the *Storch* thought the plane was beautiful.

Two things were of vital importance as designers worked to shape the plane—visibility and lift. The wings sat high on the fuselage of the *Storch*, giving flyers an unobstructed view of the ground below. The two-person cockpit was practically a greenhouse filled with a puzzle-like layout of flat, Perspex glass panes. The wide cabin even allowed a flyer to lean over in his seat and look straight down as he passed over something of interest.

The second trait made the Fi 156 most remarkable. Its massive, straight wing had a loading factor of just ten pounds per square foot. Combined with big flaps and efficient leading edge

slats, this allowed the plane to maintain lift even at very slow speeds. A *Storch* could cruise, under full control, at airspeeds down to thirty-one miles per hour. If there was a slight headwind, the plucky *Storch* could actually hover near a target as it spotted for German artillery.

The machine was so slow, in fact, that designers allowed for the wings to fold back against the fuselage. That way, even on a blustery day, the *Storch* could be moved from place to place on the battlefield on the ground.

Operating near the front lines, the short takeoff and landing abilities of the *Storch* became legendary. The plane could spring into the air from a field, a road, or any other open space in just fifty-five yards with an eight miles per hour headwind. With the same wind, the plane could touch down in an area less than half that size.

The *Storch* became something of a flying Jeep for Germany in the Spanish Civil War and then during World War II. It was

ABOVE: Like many German engines of the era, the *Storch*'s Argus As 10 is an inverted inline. The little V-8 can generate up to 240 horsepower and is cooled by air entering the scoop below in the plane's propeller hub.

used to spot for artillery, shuttle VIPs, evacuate injured men, and carry mail and messages over combat areas. Famously, a *Storch* was used to spirit away Fascist Dictator Benito Mussolini from his boulder-strewn mountaintop prison near Gran Sasso in 1943.

The FHC *Storch* is one of five Fi-156s restored under the ownership of Jan Mueller of Canton, Michigan. Mueller took over a project started by an acquaintance who had acquired the first of the *Storch* aircraft in France in the late 1970s. Mueller decided to expand the project and engaged his friend to return to Europe and find more *Storch* aircraft and parts. At the same time, Mueller hired Bruce Panzl to set up a rebuilding operation at Mettetal Airport in Plymouth, Michigan. Altogether, two German and three French *Storch* aircraft were rebuilt.

The restoration of the first four aircraft took some eleven years, culminating in the showing of three at the Experimental Aircraft Association (EAA) Fly-in in August 1990. The FHC

aircraft was registered with the FAA on October 18, 1989, but it was not one of the three flown to the EAA event. An article of the time says "[the fourth] had to be left behind because of an eleventh hour engine problem." The FHC purchased the aircraft on December 5, 2000.

The *Storch* was a C-2 version built in Kassel at the Fieseler factory on November 24, 1939. The aircraft is painted in a standard splinter camouflage with the distinctive yellow bands on the fuselage and wing tips signifying service on the Eastern Front. The 2E + RA *Verbandskennzeichen* (operational code) indicates that this is aircraft "R" of the wing headquarters of bomber wing 54. This unit participated in the first stages of

continued on page 174

LEFT: While some aircraft have leading edge slats that deploy at low speeds to help with maneuverability, the *Storch*'s speed, relatively, is always slow. Therefore, the Fieseler designers equipped the plane with fixed slats. This system spans the plane's entire long wing and helps the aircraft take off and land in incredibly short distances.

BELOW LEFT: This straight-down view gives a good look into the roomy and mostly transparent cabin of the Fieseler *Storch*. All the glass served a purpose as a pilot scouted from the air, but FHC pilots say the cockpit offers no relief from the sun on a hot day.

BELOW RIGHT: The venerable *Storch* needed some type of protection as it flew over the battlefield. The rear-seater could turn around and take on any enemy flyer who gave chase with his MG 15. The back wall of the plane was covered with spare drums of ammunition for the machine gun.

ABOVE: You can't beat the view from the pilot's seat of the *Storch*. The greenhouse cockpit was made for the flyer, operating as a spotter for German artillery or scouting for his unit. Slanted panes at his elbows even allowed the crew to lean over and look straight down.

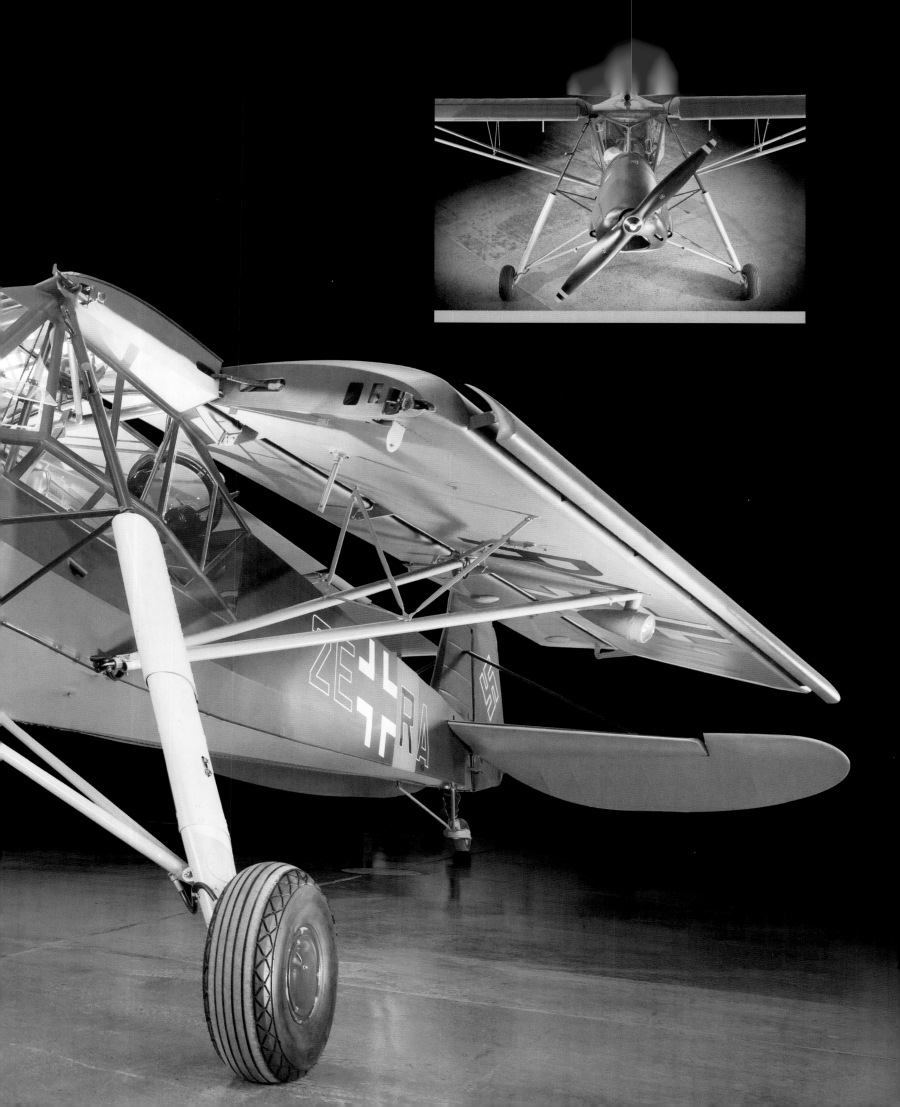

continued from page 169

Operation Barbarossa, the Nazi invasion of Russia, through December 1941.

Another plane in the FHC took a more direct role in the fighting on the ground. The famous Ilyushin Il-2 *Shturmovik* was produced in epic numbers in the Soviet Union during World War II and flew on the Eastern Front against Nazi Germany. The heavily armored aircraft was designed to operate close to the ground and attack enemy troops, tanks, and trucks.

The first example of this aircraft type flew in 1939. While the aft part of the fuselage was made of wood, the forward half was heavily armored. The vital areas of the plane—pilot, engine, and fuel tank—were shrouded in armor plate for protection against ground fire. The plane carried machine guns, heavy cannon, and bombs on internal and on external racks.

Very few Il-2s had entered service by the start of the Nazi invasion of the Soviet Union. As Germany threatened Moscow and other cities in western Russia, many Soviet aircraft factories were moved eastward over the Ural Mountains. When Stalin was not getting the desired production rates from Ilyushin and Mikoyan-Gurevich, a fighter builder, he sent telegrams to factory managers:

> You have let down our country and our Red Army. You have the nerve not to manufacture Il-2s until now. Our Red Army now needs Il-2 aircraft like the air it breathes, like the bread it eats. Shenkman produces one Il-2 a day and Tretyakov builds one or two MiG-3s daily. It is a mockery of our country and the Red Army. I ask you not to try the government's patience, and demand that you manufacture more Ils. This is my final warning.—Stalin

Production, of course, increased dramatically, so much so that, if you add the number of up-rated Il-10s to those of the Il-2, the Il-2-type aircraft becomes the single most-produced military aircraft design in all of aviation history.

TOP: A nose-on view shows how the *Storch* got its nickname. The plane's long, gangly landing gear was reminiscent of a stork's long legs as it landed on a rooftop.

ABOVE: As much as you can in the big-winged *Storch*, a German pilot shows off for the camera in this 1940s publicity photo. While the FHC's aircraft is equipped with a tail wheel, this version of the liaison plane has a tail skid for operating from grass fields.

PREVIOUS PAGES: The *Storch*'s wings fold back to help crews hide the plane close to the front lines and to allow men to move it via road or rail. When the FHC's hangar becomes crowded, mechanics sometimes fold the wings of the plane to allow a bit more space in the exhibit area. INSET: The Fieseler *Storch* is a bit on the homely side but it was tremendously successful at its job. The planes were so unique, simple, and capable that when Allied units captured them, they often used the aircraft as their own. It's fair to say that the *Storch* was not pretty, it was practical.

ABOVE: The Il-2 is equipped with a dependable Allison V-1710-113 12-cylinder engine. The left-hand turning power plant and propeller came from a P-38 Lightning fighter.

FOLLOWING PAGES: The FHC's Il-2M3 is the only flying example of the type left in the world today. It is also the only *Shturmovik* currently on display in the Western Hemisphere. INSET: Considered an icon in Russia, the famous *Shturmovik* helped turn the tide on the Eastern Front by hammering German tanks and troops from the air.

The Soviets needed them, too. Flying ground attack missions against seasoned German gun, plane, and tank crews led to the loss of thousands of Red Army planes each year. The somewhat inflated Luftwaffe claims for Il-2 aircraft destroyed in 1943 and 1944 were 6,900 and 7,300 respectively.

Like Soviet T-34 tanks on the ground, legions of Il-2s overwhelmed the Germans. The enemy knew the plane as *der Schwarze Tod* (the black death). German flyers, being somewhat literal, called the plane the "hunchback." Other German aviators, well aware of the plane's legendary toughness, called the Il-2 *Betonvogel,* loosely, "the concrete bird."

The Russians had nicknames for the plane, too. Soviet pilots lovingly called the plane *Ilyusha*, like the character in the famous novel *The Brothers Karamazov*. To the Red Army on the ground, the Il-2 was "the Winged Tank" or, perhaps most endearingly of all, "the Flying Infantryman."

The Il-2 helped win the war in Russia and the plane took on an almost mythical quality, like the Spitfire did in the dark days of the Battle of Britain. Even today, the Il-2 holds a special place in the hearts of the Russian people as the fearsome tank-killing machine that helped push the Germans out of the Soviet Union.

The FHC plane is an Ilyushin Il-2M3, sometimes called an "Il-2 Type 3" or a "1944 production" Il-2. The plane has a 23mm

continued on page 180

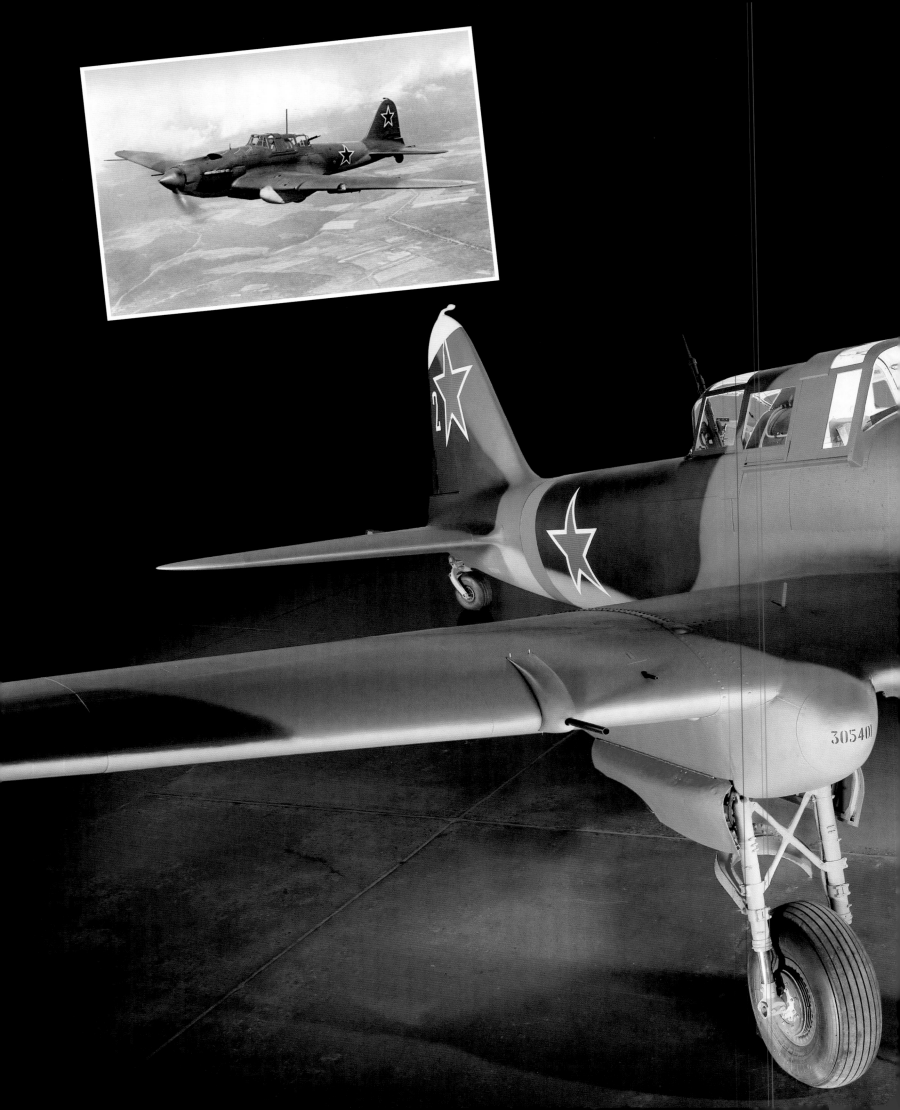

ABOVE: Russian Il-2 warplanes are photographed over Berlin in 1945. While *Shturmovik* aircraft and T-34 tanks were often outclassed by German high-tech military machines, in the end, the Soviets overwhelmed the Nazis with sheer numbers.

RIGHT: The FHC's Il-2 is photographed under construction in southwestern Siberia in December 2010. The plane was assembled in a former fighter factory by Russian craftsmen and aviation specialists.

OPPOSITE: Reports mention that direct strikes from German 20mm cannon failed to penetrate the Il-2's bulletproof wind screen. The plane's glass is faceted; when one pane was crazed by damage, the others remained unharmed, allowing the pilot to continue to fly and fight.

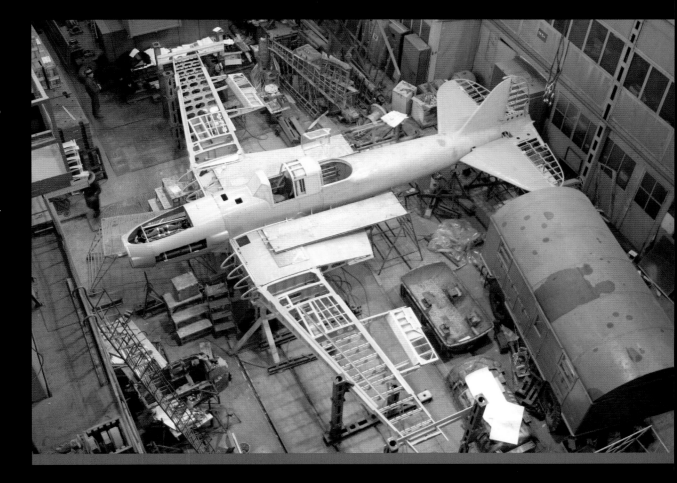

continued from page 175

cannon in each wing, as well as 7.62mm ShKAS machine guns. Designers gave the 1944 version of the plane all-metal wings and swept the planform of the outer wings aft, changing the center of gravity.

The center of gravity had been altered when a tail gunner was added to the design more than a year before. The new fifteen-degree swept-back wings transferred more lift aft, thus compensating for more weight in the rear section of the plane. As a result, the 1944 version of the attack bomber, sometimes called the "wing with arrow" model, regained some of the exceptional control of the first, single seat Il-2s.

Il-2M3 serial number 305401 was built in the city of Kuybyshev, present day Samara, in the middle of 1943. Kuybyshev was a hub of Il-2 production with multiple factories creating some twenty thousand examples of the slightly over thirty-six thousand total aircraft built. Interestingly, Kuybyshev was also chosen to be the capital of the USSR should Moscow have fallen to the invading Germans.

After construction, the plane was assigned to the 828th Attack Aviation Regiment of the 260th Composite Air Division. This unit was part of the Seventh Air Army, which supported the Soviet Red Army's Seventh Army on the lower part of the Karelian Front (along the border between Finland and the USSR).

The plane participated in more than a year of combat flying, but little is known about its particular missions and feats. The plane was most likely involved in the Svir–Petrozavodsk Offensive in the summer of 1944 against Finnish forces.

The aircraft met its end on October 10, 1944. This date corresponds to the October 7 Petsamo–Kirkenes Offensive. This major military offensive was mounted by the Red Army against the Germans in northern Finland and Norway.

OPPOSITE: Hidden from most who see the Il-2 on the ground, the plane has a large scoop on the top of its nose. Air is routed through the center of the aircraft's fuselage to a radiator near the pilot's feet. The "buried" location of the delicate radiator helps protect it from enemy fire.

ARMOR

Operating close to the enemy on the ground can be bad for your health. The designers built an armored shell around the plane's engine and pilot to help keep the Il-2 flying. The armor ranged from 4mm to 12mm thick with heavy plates held together with rivets and bolts. Some of the armor on the FHC's Il-2 still hold bullet holes and dents from combat in 1944.

It probably only took a second or two for a young man recruited to be an Il-2 gunner to recognize that he would be situated outside this armored shell meant to protect the plane's vital components. As horrifying as it sounds, gunners could be "changed out" like a crushed wingtip or burst tire. In fact, the position was so transient that no one even bothered to design a real seat for the flyer. The gunner rode on a canvas "swing" affixed to either side of the fuselage.

Wielding a heavy Berezin UBT machine gun, it was the job of the tail gunner to keep enemy fighters away while the Il-2 was making its attack runs and then heading away from the action. Never as fast as German fighters, the tail gun was a must to protect the Shturmovik.

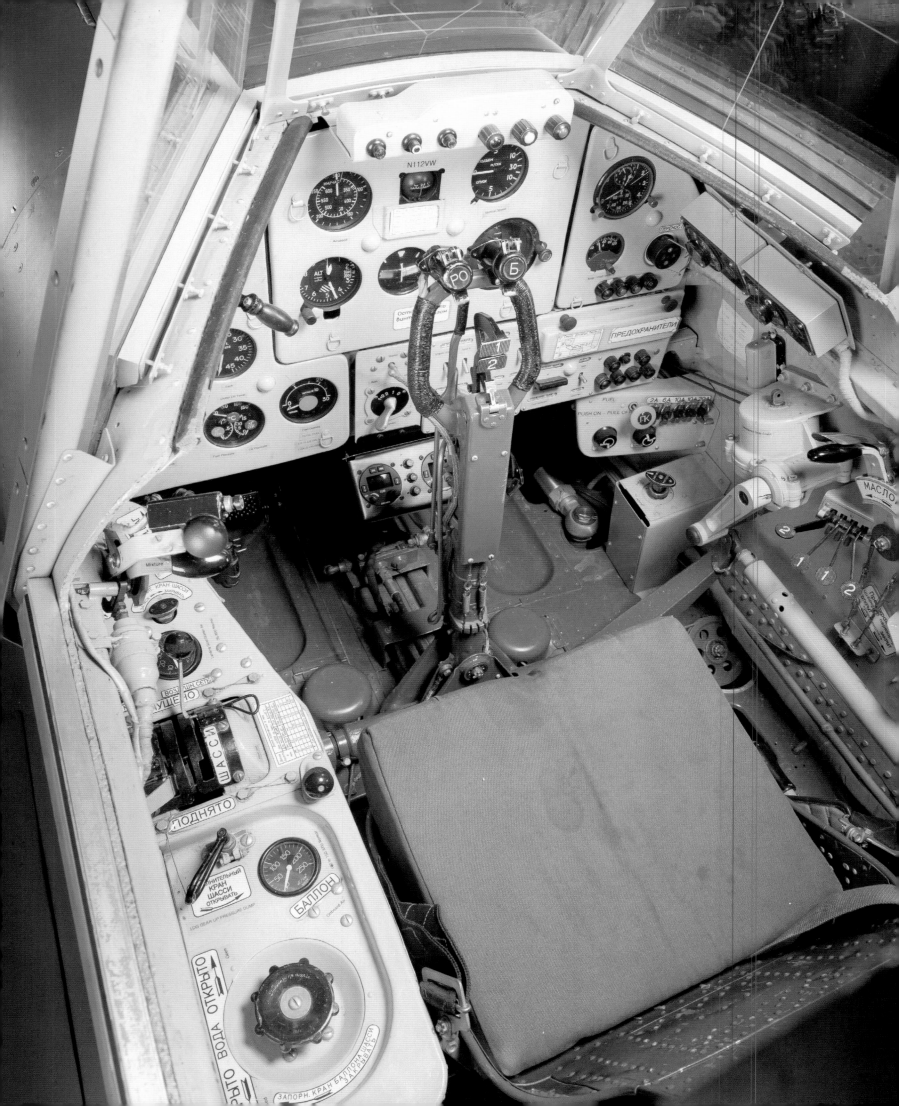

On October 10, the plane was crewed by Junior Lt. K. P. Prohorov, the pilot, and gunner S. M. Semyonov. While attacking an enemy airfield in the afternoon, some five kilometers southeast of Luostari, the plane was hit by antiaircraft fire and its engine began to smoke.

Gunner Semyonov bailed out of the plane at a low altitude and was killed when he struck the ground. Pilot Prohorov headed southeast, ran out of altitude in the vicinity of the Titovka River, and attempted to land the plane on one of the thousands of frozen lakes in the area.

The landing was a violent one, severely wounding Prohorov, who later died. The wreck was abandoned and later sank into the lake during the spring thaw.

In 1991, the crashed plane was discovered in the nameless lake by searchers scouting the area with a helicopter. The recovery crew found rockets and bombs still attached to the plane when it was raised to the surface.

Many parts from this aircraft that were still relatively intact were used in the subsequent restoration, such as the engine compartment, propeller, the central part of the fuselage, and parts of the tail. The wings had been severely damaged in the crash landing decades before and could not be used in the restoration. Restorers estimate that 60 percent of all the original parts used in the FHC aircraft project came from this wreck.

A second donor of parts came from the wreck of aircraft serial number 4283. This plane was crewed by pilot Junior Lt. Vladimir Andreevich Kurochkin and gunner Sgt. Vladimir

OPPOSITE: The instrument panel of the Il-2 has the principal flying instruments grouped in the center with engine gauges to the left. The control stick has two thumb buttons; for machine guns and cannon.

BELOW: The *Shturmovik*'s main gear was built extra tough. The burly twin struts look like those seen on cargo planes. When the gear was raised, the exposed tires acted as an anti-damage feature, should the plane be forced to land on its belly.

Sevostianovich Zenkov of the 658th Ground Attack Regiment in the 11th Mixed Air Corps. Both men were called to service from the Yaroslavl Tire Factory.

On February 12, 1944, the men and their plane did not return from a mission. It is reported that the pair intentionally crashed their damaged plane into a German antiaircraft battery near the village of Maevo in the Novocokolnicheskiy District. Both flyers were nominated for the title Hero of the Soviet Union, but received lesser awards posthumously for their heroic actions.

The plane wreck was found in Lake Trostinetz and raised. Parts from the center section and the main landing gear legs from this plane were used in the Il-2 restoration.

BELOW: The FHC's aircraft has the paint scheme of "Number 810," an aircraft that never made it home. Though 810 came from the factory bare metal, crewmen painted it in the field. They were under such pressure to get the plane flying combat missions immediately, that they never got around to painting the intricate "greenhouse" nose and cockpit areas on the aircraft.

A third source of components for the plane came from Il-2 serial number 7593 which crashed in a swampy area named Stivany near the town of Pyzhov. Flown by Grigory A. Fedirko and a gunner named I. A. Rylov, this plane was hit by antiaircraft fire. The plane crashed into the swamp on January 12, 1944.

Locals attempted a recovery as early as the 1980s, but found the plane buried too deeply in the muddy swamp. Later recovery attempts were more successful at extricating parts of the aircraft. The restorers were able to locate many parts around the cockpit area to use in the restoration. These included instrumentation, control stick, cockpit floor, and other cockpit parts.

The fourth and final wreck used to restore the FHC plane came from another swamp. This 724th Air Attack Regiment aircraft was reported missing on February 1, 1944, in the area of Maevo–Alushkovo. In the 1950s, the wreck was discovered along with the body of the gunner, Sgt. Alexey Alexandrovich Titov. Searchers at that time thought Titov was the pilot of a

one-man fighter aircraft, and the wreck stayed undisturbed until researchers uncovered the fact that Titov was actually part of an Il-2 pilot and gunner team.

Much later, Lt. Alexander Sabirovich Sabdarov, the pilot, and more of the wrecked aircraft were recovered from the long-ignored crash site. Restorers were able to recover parts of the plane's armored fuselage and armored cowlings from the wreck. The cowlings still showed bullet holes from combat that took place decades before.

A specialist firm in Novosibirsk, Russia, called Retro Avia Tech Ltd. collected the parts from each of these original Il-2 aircraft. The company's head, Boris Osentinsky, is well known in the warbird community for past restorations including I-16 and MiG-3 fighter aircraft. The idea of creating an Il-2 restoration was conceived in the early 2000s and a contract was signed with the FHC in 2005.

The original parts, acquired from the wrecks, were combined with new-build wooden parts, made from birch and pine, manufactured from plywood produced in Finland.

It has been decades since anyone has been able to get an Il-2 engine, the Mikulin AM-38F, to function. So, the FHC aircraft flies with a left-turning Allison V-1710-113 engine from a P-38 Lighting fighter producing 1,475-horsepower.

The plane is painted in the colors of Air Marshal Alexander Efimov of the 298th Air Division, who flew Il-2s in combat during World War II and was twice-awarded Hero of the Soviet Union. Efimov is known not only for destroying 126 enemy tanks, but also for engaging flying German aircraft with his heavy attack plane. When Germany surrendered, he had flown 288 combat missions and destroyed seven enemy planes in air-to-air combat. Efimov passed away in Moscow in 2012.

The plane made its maiden flight in Russia in late September of 2011. Later, the plane was returned to Samara (formerly Kuybyshev) and was flown in a parade on November 7, 2011. This celebration came exactly seventy years after Red Army parades in both Moscow and Kuybyshev during World War II.

After the celebration in Russia, the plane travelled by ship to the United States. The plane flew for the first time in the United States with Steve Hinton at the controls on August 9, 2012. The FHC Il-2 is the only example of a flyable *Shturmovik* in the world today.

The planes that would become the B-26 and B-25 twin-engine medium bombers both evolved from a specification

ABOVE: A pair of B-25s cruises toward a target in the skies over Italy. The B-25 was known to be tough. The plane's double tail not only offered stability on bomb runs, it allowed a Mitchell to return home even if one vertical was completely blown off by ground fire.

circulated by the army air corps in March 1938. Though never as good-looking or speedy as the Martin B-26, North American Aviation's (NAA) B-25 outlasted its counterpart and was considered by many an archetypal American warplane.

Like a trusty tool, good looks do not always symbolize a plane's value. However, first versions of NAA's bomber were hideous. The NA-40 was a boxy-looking aircraft with a deep fuselage, twin tails, and a long, thin cockpit. Though the prototype was destroyed in a non-fatal crash during evaluation, the Army asked North American to continue development—with a few changes.

The new plane, called NA-62, had a wider fuselage, relocated wings, and new engines, but retained the distinctive double tail of the earlier model. Dual tails allowed the aircraft to be more stable and maneuverable at low speeds, because the rudders were directly aft of the engines. The double tails also provided redundancy should one vertical get damaged in combat.

The new version of the aircraft was accepted by the army while it was still yet to be built or flown. The order for 184 aircraft came ten days after Germany invaded Poland in 1939. First versions of the B-25 had wings that slanted upward, described by aeronautical engineers as dihedral. On simulated bomb runs, the plane was slightly less stable than army

evaluators wanted, so designers landed on the B-25's distinctive "gull wing" front profile. NAA designers kept the dihedral angle from the fuselage to the engines, but reduced the angle in the outboard wing.

Soon, the B-25 was given the nickname "Mitchell," in honor of William "Billy" Mitchell, an army general who was a strong proponent of air power in the 1920s and beyond. The B-25 Mitchell was an incredibly versatile plane. When war began for the United States, B-25s were in service almost everywhere—the Pacific, Africa, Alaska, and Europe with the RAF. Later in the war, the B-25 would serve with many other Allied nations including Australia, Russia, China, and the Netherlands.

Perhaps the most famous example of the Mitchell's ability to "do anything" came early in the war when Lt. Col. James "Jimmy" Doolittle led a group of sixteen of the big bombers off the decks of the aircraft carrier USS *Hornet* near Japan in April 1942.

Whereas the faster B-26 most often flew with army air forces units based in England, the versatile and tough B-25 was the medium bomber of choice in rougher environs such as North Africa, the Pacific, and China-Burma-India. The valuable and useful plane soon took on new roles. The navy used them as patrol bombers, another version was packed with cameras for photo missions, and others were used as training planes and transports.

Perhaps the most notable change in roles for the B-25 came when crews began to use them as attack planes. An arsenal of machine guns could be carried in the nose and forward fuselage. For example, the FHC B-25 can bring to bear nine .50-caliber forward-facing machine guns on a ground target.

PREVIOUS PAGES: The FHC's North American B-25J Mitchell was a Canadian fire bomber—equipped to drop water on forest fires—before it was restored. Today it flies in the scheme of aircraft 810 of the 490th Bomb Squadron, the "Burma Bridge Busters."

BELOW: After a long trip from southern California, the FHC's Mitchell touches down at Paine Field. A pair of flyers ferried the plane from the restoration shop to its permanent home in 2011. The arrival of the biggest and most complex World War II aircraft in the collection was followed up with a large crate filled with spare parts and a bevy of vintage manuals.

OPPOSITE, TOP: The FHC's B-25J is fully restored to its World War II configuration, including a full complement of equipment in the cockpit. On the left is the pilot's N-3C gunsight along with an old style ring and bead sight. On the right, the co-pilot, operating as the bomber's navigator, used the plane's astrocompass. Over his right ear is the B-25's gun camera.

OPPOSITE, BOTTOM: Crawling through a small tunnel gave flyers access to the B-25's greenhouse nose. The cramped space is filled with guns, ammunition boxes and feeds, oxygen bottle, armor, and the plane's bomb sight.

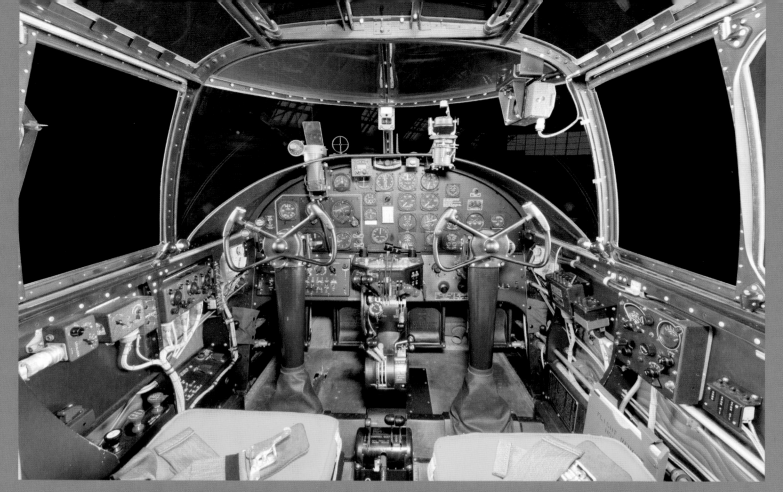

In the Pacific and China-Burma-India, B-25s blasted enemy ships, bridges, and airfields with this overwhelming firepower. One version of the aircraft even carried a heavy 75mm gun in the nose.

The FHC B-25J was built in Kansas City and accepted by the army air forces on December 28, 1944. Two days later, it was delivered to the Air Transport Command in Mobile, Alabama. The plane was then transferred to the Air Material Command at South Plains, Texas in March 1945. In July 1947, it was moved to Robins Air Force Base in Georgia.

Unlike other World War II aircraft that were scrapped at the end of the war, the B-25 continued to be operated by both military units, like the Air National Guard, and civilian operators—a testament to the versatility of the plane's design. The FHC B-25 was one of 117 to be modified by the Aircraft Division of Hughes Tool Company in Culver City, California for use as radar fighter control trainers in 1951. Modifications included the installation of the E-1 fire control system in the bomb bay, a nose mounted radome, and the addition of an astrodome in the navigator's area.

Now designated a TB-25K, the aircraft was provided to the Royal Canadian Air Force (RCAF) in November 1951 under the Mutual Defense Assistance program. The plane's period with the RCAF included training of fighter backseaters to operate radar systems. The plane served in Ontario, Alberta, and Manitoba for nearly ten years.

BELOW: The B-25's bomb bay is fully-equipped and operational. A panel in the plane's nose controls the sequence and timing of the bomb release mechanisms installed in the belly of the aircraft. A common load for the Mitchell during World War II was six 500-pound bombs.

PREVIOUS PAGES: They say you can tell whether a B-25 flyer was a pilot or co-pilot by finding out which one of his ears no longer works. The plane's prop blades whirl right outside the cockpit window and the Mitchell's notoriously loud "short stack" exhaust system surrounds the bomber's two Cyclone engines just a few feet away. INSET: Part of the B-25's defensive firepower was its tail and top turrets. Each unit was equipped with a pair of .50-caliber machine guns. The tail was powered by the plane's hydraulic system while the upper turret used electrical motors. The top turret had automatic trigger cut-offs that kept the guns from shooting through the Mitchell's spinning propellers or into its twin vertical tails.

WINGED SKULL

The distinctive emblem of the 490th Bomb Squadron adorns both sides of the nose of the FHC B-25J. The artwork was developed in the early 1930s by army engineer Eugene Clay and painted on the nose of a Lockheed Hudson ferried into the Pacific by Col. James A. Philpott, the first commander of the 490th. The image, always with a fearsome skull and a set of Army Air Corps pilot's wings in a white and black circle, was used throughout World War II but was never officially accepted by the Army Air Forces as the emblem of the "Burma Bridge Busters."

By November 1961, the plane was declared surplus and transferred to Crown Assets Disposal Corporation for sale. In 1962 or 1963, Cascade Drilling Company of Alberta purchased the aircraft and converted it to a water bomber. The FHC B-25 was reportedly the first to be converted in Canada for firefighting. Due to a series of B-25 tanker crashes in the United States and a US Fire Service ruling excluding the B-25 from contracts after 1962, Cascade failed to generate any business.

Cascade sold the aircraft to Air Spray Ltd. of Edmonton, Alberta, in 1964 and it was sold again in 1967 to Northwestern Air Lease Ltd. With Northwestern, the B-25 fought fires in all the western provinces of Canada. Northwestern management sold all of their B-25s to G&M Air Lease Ltd. of St. Albert, Alberta, in 1981.

The FHC B-25 was flown as a fire tanker into the 1990s until the Canadian government decided to contract for other types of aircraft. The plane was removed from the register and exported to the United States on June 19, 1995.

The FHC purchased the plane in late 1998 and moved it to Aero Trader in Chino, California—a company well known for Mitchell bomber restorations. Aero Trader worked to convert the plane to its wartime configuration and locate and reinstall all of its long-lost equipment. The plane became one of the most accurately-restored World War II bombers in the world and is complete with guns, ammunition boxes and chutes, bomb site, oxygen bottles, armor plate, rescue equipment, astro-compass, and a thousand other items worked into a cramped,

ABOVE: Outside the FHC's main hangar, mechanics rattle the windows with a thundering engine run. Unlike B-25s that have been modified to quiet the engines and provide carburetor heat, the FHC's bomber has simple, loud, World War II-era "short stack" exhausts.

combat-era bomber interior. The aircraft was finished in 2011 and flown to Everett in June of that year.

Since the FHC B-25 never saw combat, staffers chose to pick the paint scheme of an aircraft that never came home. "Number 810" of the 490th Bomb Squadron, nicknamed the "Burma Bridge Busters," flew 116 missions in the China-Burma-India Theater during World War II. This veteran aircraft was lost in combat on May 30, 1945, when it crashed while attacking Sincheng Bridge in China.

The FHC's Republic P-47D Thunderbolt served in the United States and Brazil before its full restoration. Today, the rare survivor periodically takes to the skies to dazzle Fly Day audiences.

THE
BRUISERS

8

REPUBLIC P-47D THUNDERBOLT

GRUMMAN F6F-5 HELLCAT

The Republic P-47 Thunderbolt and Grumman F6F Hellcat were fighters cut from the same cloth. Both were designed in Long Island, New York, and the pair represented the pinnacle of American industrial might. Built around the same big, air-cooled Pratt & Whitney R-2800 engine, the duo were generally the same size and shape, one serving the US Army and the other the navy.

Made solid, heavy, and powerful, the two fighters were well known for their ability to absorb great punishment and still return home. The two planes dominated the skies by taking on aerial foes and made life miserable for Axis ground forces during the last years of the war.

The P-47 Thunderbolt came first. The US military was influenced by fighter designs like the Spitfire and Bf 109, and the army needed better aircraft to take on potential enemies in air-to-air combat. When Republic's Russian-born designer Alexander Kartveli met with army air corps officials in June 1940, he came away with an intimidating set of requirements. They wanted speed, heavy armament, great protection (armor and self-sealing fuel tanks), and exceptional range. It was clear that nothing Republic had in the air, or even on the drawing board, would do.

The plane that Kartveli and his crew designed was a large, heavy interceptor. The XP-47B made its maiden flight on May 6, 1941. The heart of the new machine was its Double Wasp engine, which had been used in the Vought F4U Corsair naval fighter a year before. The eighteen-cylinder behemoth made the Corsair America's first single-engine fighter capable of flying at more than four hundred miles per hour.

ABOVE: Turning to chase a ferry boat across Puget Sound, FHC pilot "Bud" Granley puts the Thunderbolt through its paces during a test flight not far from the Flying Heritage Collection's home at Paine Field.

While the R-2800 was the heart of the Thunderbolt, the turbo supercharger was its lungs. This device, located behind the wings, collected and compressed lighter high-altitude air and then fed the engine denser, sea-level-like air for better performance at higher altitudes.

The lines of the P-47 were scribed around this union between its power plant and turbo supercharger. More accurately, the Thunderbolt got its "jug" shape from the maze of air ducts in its belly that funneled air from nose to tail and back again. The turbo supercharger was driven by exhaust gases from the engine. Clean, cool air was scooped from a large opening under the engine. Some of this air was used to cool

oil, while the rest was compressed, then cooled, then sent back to the R-2800 in the nose. Each function required a complex duct system to move air through the fuselage.

In service, pilots and ground crew liked the duct system in the belly of the fighter because it protected a flyer in hard, wheels-up landings, and the "crush zone" protected vital parts of the aircraft, allowing it to be repaired quickly.

The other thing that pilots adored about the P-47 was its heavy complement of guns. The designers were able to shoehorn eight .50-caliber guns into the wings by creating an ingenious mechanical system to compress the landing gear when stowed. This fit the needs of a new era of air-to-air combat that stressed incredible punching power to violently and quickly smash enemy aircraft.

However, American pilots did not immediately accept the first P-47s when they first arrived in Europe in April 1943. The

Thunderbolt, or as flyers called it, "the Jug," was a monster. Used to nimble planes like the Spitfire, the P-47 seemed like a delivery truck.

The size of the P-47, though, allowed it to fly much farther than a Spitfire. The Jug would be used most often in the early days as an escort plane, despite having been built as an interceptor. The P-47 could carry 305 gallons of fuel in the fuselage along with external drop tanks, too. This fuel load allowed the P-47 escorts to stay with the bombers and battle Luftwaffe interceptors for far longer than Spitfires.

When long-endurance Mustangs arrived on the scene to escort American bombers, many P-47s switched roles again. The timing could not have been better. As Allied troops stormed ashore in France, Jugs took on the job of ground attack. The P-47 was uniquely suited for the task—burly airframe, heavy guns, and a durable engine.

ABOVE: As the FHC's P-47 turns for home and exposes its belly, one can see the outlet for the plane's turbo supercharger just forward of the fighter's tail wheel. The heavy piece of equipment was located here to give the Jug better balance and to maximize the pilot's view from the cockpit.

Above all, the Thunderbolt was known to be almost supernaturally tough. Tales of Jugs that had buzz-sawed through the trees, smashed into the side of a German truck, or came home with an engine cylinder completely shot away were often more truth than fiction. Pilots grew to love the P-47, because it nearly always gave them a fighting chance to make it back to base.

The FHC P-47D-40-RA Thunderbolt was built in Evansville, Indiana, in the last months of World War II. According to the *Army Air Forces Statistical Digest*, the US Government acquired the plane for around $83,001.00.

Evansville was the second Republic factory building P-47s, the other site being Farmingdale in Long Island, New York.

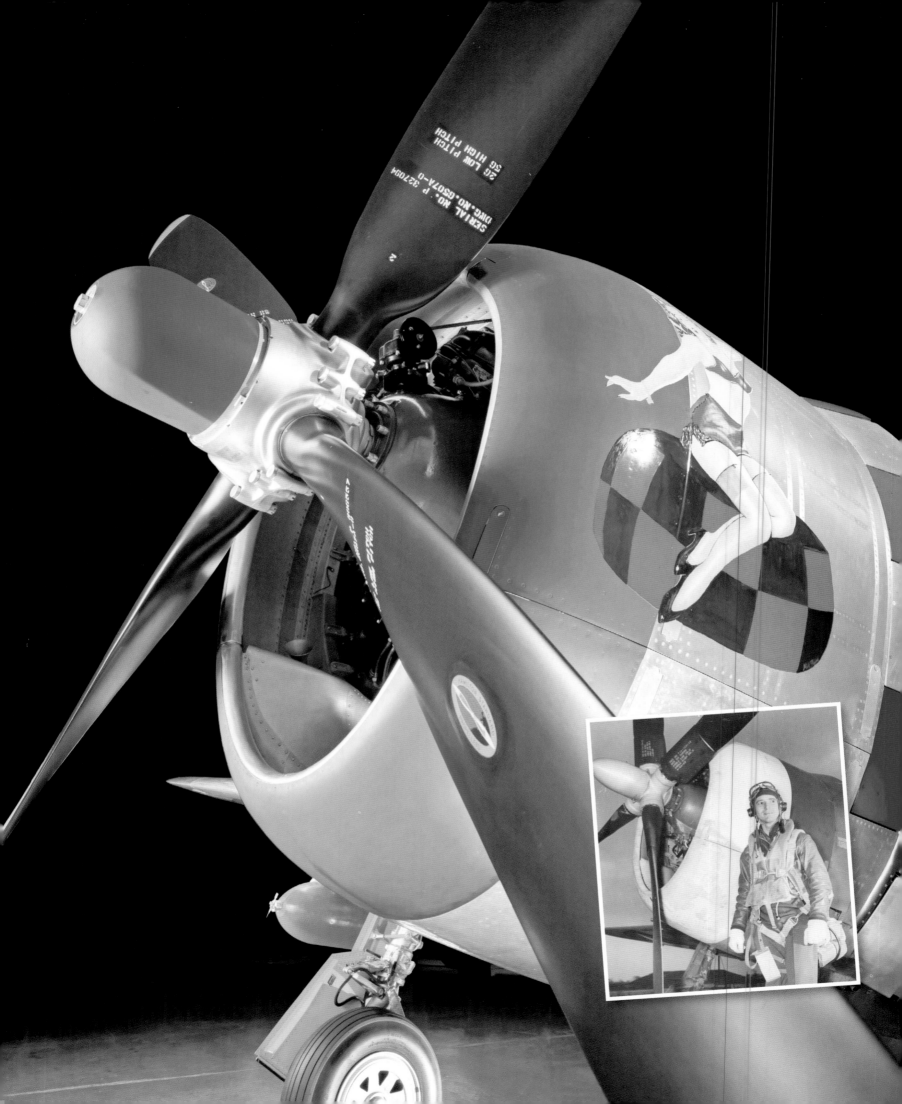

SERIAL NO. P 327094
DWG. NO. G507A-0
26 LOW PITCH   26 HIGH PITCH

This second factory was built inland, which was thought to be out of range of even the boldest Nazi bombing attacks. The first P-47s left the Evansville factory as the building was still being constructed in mid-1942. In total, the Indiana plant built 6,242 of the 15,683 Thunderbolts produced.

The FHC aircraft was delivered to the army and accepted on June 27, 1945. It was almost immediately put into storage. While the plane was at Tinker Army Air Field in Oklahoma, the US Army Air Forces became the US Air Force. As well, the Thunderbolt's designation changed from P-47, for "Pursuit," to F-47, for "Fighter."

From 1948 to 1953, the Thunderbolt served Air National Guard and Strategic Air Command units in New York, New Jersey, Pennsylvania, Georgia, and Kentucky. By April 1953,

the FHC's F-47 had been moved back into storage, presumably for eventual transfer to a Latin American country. The plane was, in fact, acquired by Brazil's *Força Aérea Brasileira* (FAB) in September 1953.

Brazilian pilots had flown P-47s since combat in Italy during World War II. By early 1952, around fifty-one P-47/F-47s had been supplied to Brazil through Lend-Lease agreements.

OPPOSITE: The monstrous snout of the Thunderbolt sometimes gets in the way. On the ground, a Jug pilot has no chance of seeing anything directly in front of him for a hundred yards or more. A mechanic would often sit on the wing of the fighter, giving a flyer a second pair of eyes until right before takeoff.INSET: The Republic P-47 was a staggeringly large aircraft. Here, Maj. Walter Beckham, ace of the 353rd Fighter Group, poses with his trusty Jug. Noses of early P-47s were often painted white to avoid confusion with German radial-engine Fw 190 fighters.

CAPACIOUS COCKPIT

While the size of the average man stayed about the same, the size of the average fighter plane and cockpit increased during World War II. This image shows the spacious working space in the FHC's P-47 Thunderbolt. It is not surprising that the interior of America's biggest single engine fighter of the war had the largest cockpit, too. It was so commodious, in fact, that it caused pilots of all nations to take notice. Pilots who transitioned from flying Spitfires in RAF Eagle Squadrons were shocked by the size of the plane. Compared to flying in the cozy cockpit of Supermarine's bantam defensive fighter, the inside of the Jug seemed disturbingly roomy. British observers noted wryly that one might slip off the seat, fall to the cockpit floor, and really get hurt. The Germans were puzzled by the Thunderbolt's interior, as well, when they inspected a captured P-47. Luftwaffe Gen. Adolf Galland wrote that the cockpit was big enough to walk around in. Other German pilots, used to the comfy if-not-cramped cockpit of the Bf 109, felt that everything was out of reach. Another speculated that a pilot might be able to dodge bullets simply by loosening his shoulder straps and leaning to one side or the other as he flew.

Both Allied and Axis pilots were startled by the size of the Thunderbolt's spacious cockpit. Compared to the cramped quarters of the Bf 109 or Spitfire, the inside of a Jug seemed like a ballroom. Most flyers found the extra space oddly disturbing.

ABOVE: The P-47 is equipped with a K-14 gyroscopic gunsight. In the manual, it is described as "the answer to a poor deflection shooter's prayer." The unit worked as a fixed sight or the gyro could be engaged to account for the maneuvers of the Thunderbolt and its prey in aerial combat.

PREVIOUS PAGES: The FHC's P-47D carries a painting of *Tallahassee Lassie*, the wife of pilot Ralph Jenkins. The image was created by 510th Fighter Squadron artist Staff Sgt. Lynn Trank, jokingly considered, "the only indispensable man in the squadron." INSET: Seattleite Capt. Ralph C. Jenkins poses in the cockpit of one of his P-47 aircraft during World War II. Though he was never hit in combat, his name appeared on the canopy rail of a number of Thunderbolts during his time in the service. Each plane had the same name painted on the cowling—*Tallahassee Lassie*.

speed" versus the Zero. The Hellcat would change all that. Grumman's new F6F would be bigger, faster, and more powerful than the vaunted Mitsubishi Zero.

Incorporating the R-2800 engine into the new aircraft design meant building a whole new airframe. In actuality, the Hellcat wasn't an improved Wildcat; it was the next generation of naval fighter. In the process, Grumman listened to naval aviators' comments and did away with many of the Wildcat's weaknesses, while keeping its strengths. The Hellcat's big engine meant that the Wildcat's odd, manually operated scissor landing gear had to go. The new, wide-stance, more conventional gear allowed the plane's Pratt & Whitney to turn a giant thirteen-foot one-inch Hydromatic propeller. Even little things were changed. The Wildcat had aggravating pull handles to charge the plane's machine guns. With the Hellcat, a flyer just flipped a switch.

In many respects, the Hellcat was nearly always easy on an aviator. By comparison, the Vought F4U Corsair seemed like a high-strung predator, always ready to turn on its master. The Hellcat was really a pussycat at heart. For a carrier landing, the Corsair had questionable visibility and wicked stall tendencies. A Hellcat flyer sat high, able to see over the fighter's massive nose, and the plane had no hidden quirks in the skies or in the landing pattern. The F6F was a big, lovable lug that did what it was asked to do, without complaint.

Of course, operating from carriers, the F6F had folding wings. While many of the Wildcat's aggravating characteristics went away, Grumman kept the good ones. The Sto-Wing concept, initiated by Leroy Grumman himself using a paperclip and eraser as his model, allowed five "folded" planes to fit into space of two fixed-wing fighters. Developed for the Wildcat, the system was transferred to the bigger Hellcat.

The first Hellcat flew on June 26, 1942. Amazingly, three months later the fighter was ready for mass production. Fifteen months after that, Grumman had 25,094 employees and had built more than 2,500 Hellcats.

Hellcats went to war on August 31, 1943, over Marcus Island. Quickly, the aircraft became the dominant fighter in the Pacific by dethroning the once seemingly unbeatable Zero. Beyond tangles with Japanese fighters, the Hellcat earned a reputation as a valuable attack plane. As US forces hopped from island to island and the Japanese air presence faded, the dependable and versatile Hellcat lugged bombs into the skies to batter enemy airfields and fortifications.

As with the P-47 Thunderbolt, the Hellcat could take punishment and dish it out. Flyers sometimes called it the "Aluminum Tank" and joked that Grumman had used steel girders from New York's abandoned Second Avenue elevated railroad to make the planes.

In an illustration of how tough the Hellcat was, the navy required Grumman to "drop-test" a new F6F airframe. Engineers calculated that the nineteen-feet-per-second drop to the pitching deck of a carrier during landing could be replicated with a straight drop of ten feet. They lifted the plane up and let it go. The Hellcat simply bounced to a stop with no ill effects. At the end of the test, Grumman's engineers decided to have a little fun with their test subject. They winched the plane up to the ceiling in their test facility—twenty-one feet—and let the plane fall. Again, the burly Hellcat bounced and then settled to the cement floor below, unharmed.

The FHC Hellcat was built in Bethpage, New York, and accepted by the navy on May 17, 1945. It was a F6F-5N night fighter equipped with a radar and special instrumentation. The plane was assigned to the Carrier Aircraft Service Unit 1 on Ford Island, Pearl Harbor, Hawaii, from July to September 1945.

In 1945 and 1946, the fighter was in the general pool at Pearl Harbor and Alameda. Then, the FHC Hellcat went into a period of storage in a blimp hangar at NAS Glynco in Georgia from August 1946 to June 1948.

Through 1950 and 1951, the plane was moved to a Naval Air Reserve Training unit in New York. After that, the Hellcat was assigned to the Fleet All Weather Training Unit at Barbers

ABOVE: FHC test pilot Steve Hinton takes the newly restored Grumman fighter to the skies in 2013. The plane was on display for years in the FHC's hangar before being put back into flying shape by collection staffers. Today it is one of the FHC's most popular planes.

PREVIOUS PAGES: The FHC's Grumman F6F-5 Hellcat was miraculously saved from destruction during its years serving as a remote control drone. It is one of just a handful of Hellcats flying in the world today. INSET: Condensation rings stream from the propeller blades of an F6F-3 Hellcat aboard the USS *Yorktown* in 1943. The image was taken as the Grumman fighters entered combat for the first time, against targets on Marcus Island.

Point, Hawaii, from June 1952 to February 1954. Then, there were brief stops in Alameda, Norfolk, and Litchfield Park, in Arizona, before the plane's conversion to a drone in 1957.

The plane was flown with utility unit VU-3 from Brown Field, California, in 1958, before spending its final military years with the Research and Development unit at the Naval Air Facility at China Lake.

The FHC Hellcat's last military flight, under the controls of a pilot named Hemming, was on October 4, 1961, terminating at Bethpage on Long Island, New York. The fighter had accumulated 856 hours of flying time while in navy service.

The FHC Hellcat appears to have been the last, or next to last Hellcat used by the navy. The monthly *Allowances and Location of Navy Aircraft* shows two remaining Hellcat drones in October 1961 with one "awaiting decision on strike." The November 1961 report does not list any Hellcats.

The US Naval Aviation Museum (NAM) in Pensacola, Florida, acquired the aircraft as a gift from Grumman Aircraft Engineering Corporation on March 15, 1965. NAM stored the Hellcat, still in the insignia red paint scheme, from China Lake, at Chevalier Field in Pensacola. It is apparent that no restoration work was done at NAM, because the

Officer in Charge of the museum, Grover Walker, is on record as requesting a trade for an exhibit-ready Hellcat. The trade was consummated on July 14, 1971, between NAM and three partners of Aerial Classics of Atlanta. The museum received BuNo 94203 in exchange. Mike Rettke, the most prominent partner, had the restored aircraft registered as N79863, and he flew it at various air shows, including the EAA at Oshkosh and AirWar74 in Windsor, Ontario.

In the fall of 1985, Patriots Point and the *Yorktown* Association purchased the Hellcat from Aerial Classics for $280,000. It was dedicated to Lt. Cmdr., later Vice Adm., James "Jimmy" Flatley Jr., the wartime commander of USS *Yorktown*'s Air Group 5 in October 1985 in a ceremony on the flight deck of the *Yorktown*—now a floating museum. The aircraft was painted glossy sea blue with Flatley's markings while displayed on the hangar deck during the period at Patriots Point.

Around 1991, Patriots Point traded the Hellcat in a three-way deal with Black Shadow Aviation and the Naval Aviation Museum to obtain a nonflying F6F along with the loan of other aircraft. The FHC Hellcat moved quickly to Warbirds of Great Britain Ltd.

Doug Arnold, the owner of Warbirds of Great Britain, had been an avid aviation collector for approximately twenty-five years when he passed away in November 1992—barely a year after acquiring the Hellcat. Rumor has it that his collection was disbanded after his death, with the naval aircraft being flown to other places and the rest of the aircraft disassembled, containerized, and dispersed. It appears that the FHC Hellcat was stored in the United States from 1992 to 1996 with a company called Iron Baron Corporation in Dover, Delaware.

In 1996, Arnold's son, David, started Flying A Services and hoped to develop an aviation museum in England. The FHC Hellcat was flown back to England from the United States via Iceland. This was the last time the plane flew until 2013. The plane's log reveals a twenty-seven-hour trip from Wichita, Kansas, to North Weald, England, from August 4 to 8 in 1997. It was stored at North Weald by Flying A Services until purchased by the FHC in late 2000 and shipped to Arlington, Washington.

continued on page 214

RIGHT: Near the FHC's hangars, mechanics conduct a test on the Hellcat's big R-2800 engine. The same type of Pratt & Whitney power plant was used in the Vought F4U Corsair and Republic P-47 Thunderbolt fighters.

ABOVE: The FHC's F6F-5 Hellcat carries the paint scheme of fighter number 32, seen here in a photo taken from the island of the USS *Randolph* in 1945.

OPPOSITE: The FHC's Hellcat carries the distinctive "G-symbol" tail of a plane from the USS *Randolph*. Through many of the last months of the war, US Navy aircraft carried bold white patterns ("geometric symbols") on their tails to aid in recognition.

RIGHT: That big engine needs an equally large propeller to slice through the air. The Hellcat's three-bladed Hydromatic is over thirteen feet in diameter. Yellow tips were standard on US warplanes. They help the spinning propeller stay visible to ground crew working around the aircraft.

BELOW: Leroy Grumman got the idea for the Hellcat's backwards wing fold from watching birds. He noticed that when a bird lands, its wings fold neatly against its body, not straight up. The Sto-Wing concept keeps the plane's center of gravity low and allows it to fit in the cramped environs of a carrier's hangar deck.

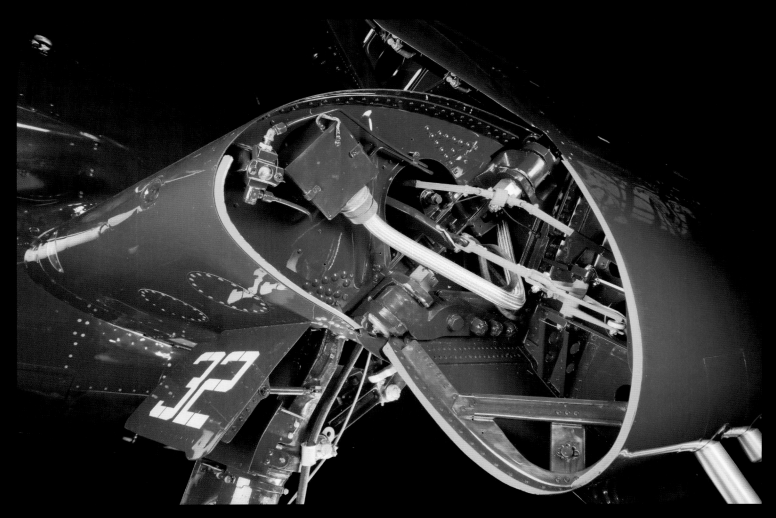

ABOVE: A Pratt &Whitney R-2800 Double Wasp radial cut-away is often displayed near the FHC's Hellcat or Thunderbolt to illustrate the monster engine behind some of the best American fighters of the war. This version came from an A-26 Invader attack bomber.

PREVIOUS PAGES: A deckhand's-eye-view of the F6F shows the big plane with its cowl flaps open. The doors on the back of the cowling could be opened or closed by the pilot to allow more or less air into the cowling and over the cylinders of the plane's air-cooled Pratt & Whitney R-2800 Double Wasp engine.

continued from page 209

During 2011 and 2012, the Hellcat went through an extensive IRAN (Inspect and Repair As Necessary) including an engine rebuild, electrical system and instrumentation restoration, control surface recovering, and painting.

The FHC Grumman F6F-5 Hellcat went into the paint shop on Valentine's Day in 2013. The scheme was chosen to honor a local ace: Lt. Reuben H. Denoff flew in the invasion of North Africa, fought with VF-9 in the Pacific, and then joined VF-12, subsequently VBF-12, aboard the aircraft carrier USS *Randolph*. Denoff finished the war with a total of five confirmed air-to-air victories. Eventually, he settled in Kennewick, Washington and worked for McDonnell Douglas Laboratories in Richland. He passed away in 1988.

The Hellcat, adorned with the *Randolph*'s distinctive striped "G-symbol" tail, flew again on March 27, 2013, with Steve Hinton as test pilot.

FLYING GUINEA PIGS

The navy had been developing drones since 1936 to perform a variety of tasks including flight-testing to avoid injury to pilots and use as targets for antiaircraft gunners. After World War II, the navy found itself with a multitude of flyable Hellcats that could be used for the strangest of assignments.

An F6F drone package included the following components: "a control unit, a radio transmitter modulator, a radio receiver-selector unit, and a relay control unit . . . and the stabilization system which includes the P-1K auto-pilot." The first two items were located on the ground or in a control aircraft while the other items were installed in the drone.

The planes were used in deadly exercises. The first F6Fs were converted in 1946 for the Bikini atom bomb tests—Operation Crossroads. The planes were plunged into the blast cloud. Those that survived the flight brought back valuable information from places manned aircraft could never safely go.

Other aircraft were used to test new antiaircraft missiles and guns, and, for each successful test, there was one less Hellcat in the Navy's inventory. Perhaps the strangest use of Hellcat drones came during the Korean War, when explosive-loaded fighters were

ABOVE: While based at the Naval Ordnance Test Station at China Lake, the FHC's Hellcat was painted red in order to keep the unpiloted drone easily in sight of its operators. The bright color also helped potential "shooters" to home in on the unmanned aircraft. Luckily, the FHC's Hellcat survived its days as a target.

flown, *kamikaze* style, into enemy bridges, tunnels, and power plant buildings. Over twelve thousand Hellcats were built, but they are a rare commodity today, partly because so many of the World War II survivors were used as flying guinea pigs.

ABOVE: In order to cross the Atlantic, many of the Hellcat's vintage instruments were switched out or discarded to install modern civilian ones. Restorers found that many of the World War II instruments were fairly easy to locate and replace. The toughest to find was the plane's eight-day clock, which was often pocketed by sailors or scrap men as a valuable souvenir.

The FHC's rare and unusual Messerschmitt Me 163 *Komet* was captured by the British at the end of World War II and evaluated by the RAF. It came to the United States from the Imperial War Museum.

THE RADICALS

MESSERSCHMITT ME 163 B-1 *KOMET*

MESSERSCHMITT ME 262 A-1A

Germany created some of the most advanced and unusual weaponry of World War II. The combination of a heritage of accomplishments in science, engineering, and craftsmanship, and Adolf Hitler's social and political agenda turned Germany into a war machine.

Hitler's ambition to "save" Germany included a willingness to fight his European neighbors on a grand scale. To do so, the people of Germany created sophisticated ships and submarines, top-of-the-line tanks and ground weapons, and some of the most advanced aircraft the world had ever known.

Perhaps one of the strangest aircraft of the conflict was the Messerschmitt Me 163 *Komet*. This tailless aircraft was the only operational warplane in history to be powered solely by a rocket engine.

It was designed by Dr. Alexander Lippisch, who had been experimenting with tailless sailplanes since 1926. The Luftwaffe transferred his group of scientists and engineers to *Messerschmitt AG* in 1939 in order to develop powered versions of their strange-looking aircraft for experimental and military use. Concurrently, other German scientists, including Werner von Braun and Hellmuth Walter, were working on rocket engines that could power aircraft.

The first Me 163, a successor to the DFS 194 powered sailplane, flew for the first time in August 1941 with a Walter RII-203b engine. The plane was fast—faster than any aircraft in the world in fact—once thundering through the skies at over 620 mph.

Continued refinements to the Me 163 included an even more powerful Walter engine designated HWK 509, which delivered over 3,700 pounds of thrust. The heart of the plane was this engine, which was fueled by a mixture of *T-stoff* (hydrogen peroxide and water) and *C-stoff* (hydrazine hydrate and methyl alcohol). This pair of dangerous chemicals became unthinkably worse when mixed and the plane's thrust came from harnessing the violent reaction between them. Beyond the fact that the fuel was corrosive and highly toxic, mistakes in ground handling or rough treatment of the aircraft during operations could, and often did, result in a massive explosion.

While the engine for the Me 163 was radical, the airframe was even moreso; a set of swept wings affixed to a rotund fuselage with no horizontal stabilizers. The fuselage was monocoque aluminum with flush rivets. The large wings were plywood, equipped with flaps, leading edge slots, and elevons—control surfaces that acted as both an elevator and an aileron.

Though unusual, the tailless Me 163 was highly maneuverable and almost impossible to stall. True to its sailplane heritage, the rocket fighter could be made to sink or spiral, but not plummet from the skies.

In order to make the aircraft as light as possible, it was launched with a main landing gear dolly that was dropped shortly after takeoff. The plane landed using a reinforced skid built into the belly of the fuselage. Pilots had to use extra care to avoid rough landings, which could set off leftover fuels in the plane's tanks.

Like everything else with this new type of plane, combat tactics had to be modified to maximize the Me 163's effectiveness. There was insufficient fuel to loiter. Messerschmitt rocket fighters had seven and a half to nine minutes of powered flight time from takeoff to fuel exhaustion.

The Me 163 could launch and climb to attack altitude in two to four minutes. Then, the pilot would approach the enemy

BELOW: While the *Komet* was noteworthy from a technological point of view, it was less than effective in combat. Hundreds of the planes were built yet they only downed a handful of enemy aircraft over Europe.

bombers from behind and below, or head-on, using his plane's superior thrust and speed to make slashing attacks with a pair of 30mm MK 108 cannon. To protect the Me 163 from the defensive fire of the bomber's machine guns, it was equipped with an armored nosecone and a 90mm-thick bullet-resistant glass windscreen panel.

The Messerschmitt Me 163 never had the impact in combat that the Luftwaffe hoped for, due to its limitations. The Luftwaffe was hopelessly outnumbered by thousands of American aircraft by the time the 163 entered the fighting. Some historians point out that the dangerous rocket plane actually killed more German aviators than American ones during the last year of war.

The FHC Me 163 carries work number 191660 and was built in late 1944 by Junkers. When the Messerschmitt factory in Regensburg-Obertraubling was bombed by the Allies, *Komet* production was moved. The Germans took the opportunity to switch the factory to production of additional Bf 109 fighters, though repairs took only a few weeks.

ABOVE: This photograph shows the FHC's Me 163 *Komet* on display at the Imperial War Museum in 1962. Note that the plane appears to have been repainted since its Luftwaffe service and is missing its blown plastic canopy.

BELOW: This *Komet* became a teaching tool and PR attraction at Freeman Field in Indiana. The little rocket plane has lost one wing so that it doesn't take up as much space in the Army's hangar. Sections of the plane's fuselage have been cut away to allow visitors to have a look at the inner workings of the captured aircraft.

Overseeing *Komet* production then fell to *Leichtflugzeugbau Klemm GmbH* in Böblingen. Sources report, "The build quality of the Klemm aircraft was much lower than those of the Messerschmitt-built examples. The relative inexperience of the Klemm company with modern metal aircraft was the main reason. The aircraft were partially built by French slave laborers, who reportedly sabotaged some of the *Komets.*"

Production management was moved again, this time to Junkers, a company with fewer projects than Messerschmitt at this late stage in the war. Over time, all production was switched to Junkers. Junkers-built 191660 took to the air for the first time on December 18, 1944, with a short flight from Brandenburg-Briest airfield to Oranienburg, Germany. The fifty-mile flight took place with the *Komet* being towed behind a powered plane and then released. Klemm chief test pilot Karl Voy glided the *Komet* to Junkers facility near Oranienburg for final tests and release to the Luftwaffe. According to the writings of a former Me 163 flyer, Voy and his colleges made at least one powered flight in each aircraft before it was delivered.

Soon after, the plane was released to *Jagdgeschwader* 400 and assigned to *Gruppe* II (II./JG 400) at Brandis, Germany, east of Leipzig. The plane was transported 143 miles to its new location most likely by truck or train. Due to fuel shortages,

II./JG 400 had very few engagements with American bombers. It is unclear whether 191660 was ever used in combat.

In March 1945, the unit was moved to Salzwedel and then to Nordholz in April. Finally, in May 1945, the unit moved to Husum in northern Germany. It was there that II./JG 400 surrendered to an RAF regiment on May 8, 1945. The British acquired most of their forty-eight intact Me 163s from this area after searching among the wrecked and parted out *Komets* and Me 262s. *Komet* number 191660 was one of 25 *Komets* airlifted to the Royal Aircraft Establishment (RAE) in Farnborough. Four others went to the French Air Force for study.

OPPOSITE, TOP: If a ground crewman accidently mixed the chemicals *C-stoff* and *T-stoff*, it was most likely the last thing he ever did. As a result, the fillers and drains on the *Komet* carry clear symbols, distinctive in color, shape, and letter, to keep anyone from inadvertently blowing themselves up, along with the valuable aircraft.

OPPOSITE, BOTTOM: This view of the belly of the *Komet* reveals the plane's unusual takeoff and landing equipment. The wheeled dolly under the plane was dropped shortly after takeoff. The ski-like skid, painted dark gray, was extended before landing and the plane would slide to a stop on grass. Also note the cable attachment point just forward of the skid—used to transport the *Komet*, unfueled, with the help of a piston-powered tow aircraft.

BIG GUN

When you are hunting big game, you need a big gun. The Messerschmitt Me 163 *Komet* carried two MK 108 autocannons. Each weapon fired 650 rounds a minute and each explosive round was over one inch in diameter. That is a lot of punching power. The American .50-caliber aircraft gun was decidedly smaller and lighter.

Making a quick and brutal attack was the only way for a *Komet* to succeed. Rocketing along, literally, at over 500 miles per hour, the Me 163 had only minutes of fuel to climb, move into position, and make a pass or two at an Allied bomber formation before gliding for home. In those rare moments—split seconds, really—where the hunter and prey were converging at almost 700 miles per hour, a peashooter was not going to cut it. You needed a knockout blow.

ABOVE: This cutaway drawing, created by the US Army Air Forces, shows the Komet's pair of bomber-busting guns, buried in the bantam fighter's thick wings. Each Mk 108 cannon could spit out ten 30mm high-explosive or high-explosive incendiary shells per second. Commonly, a Komet carried sixty rounds, per gun, into combat.

Schleppseil
hier einhängen

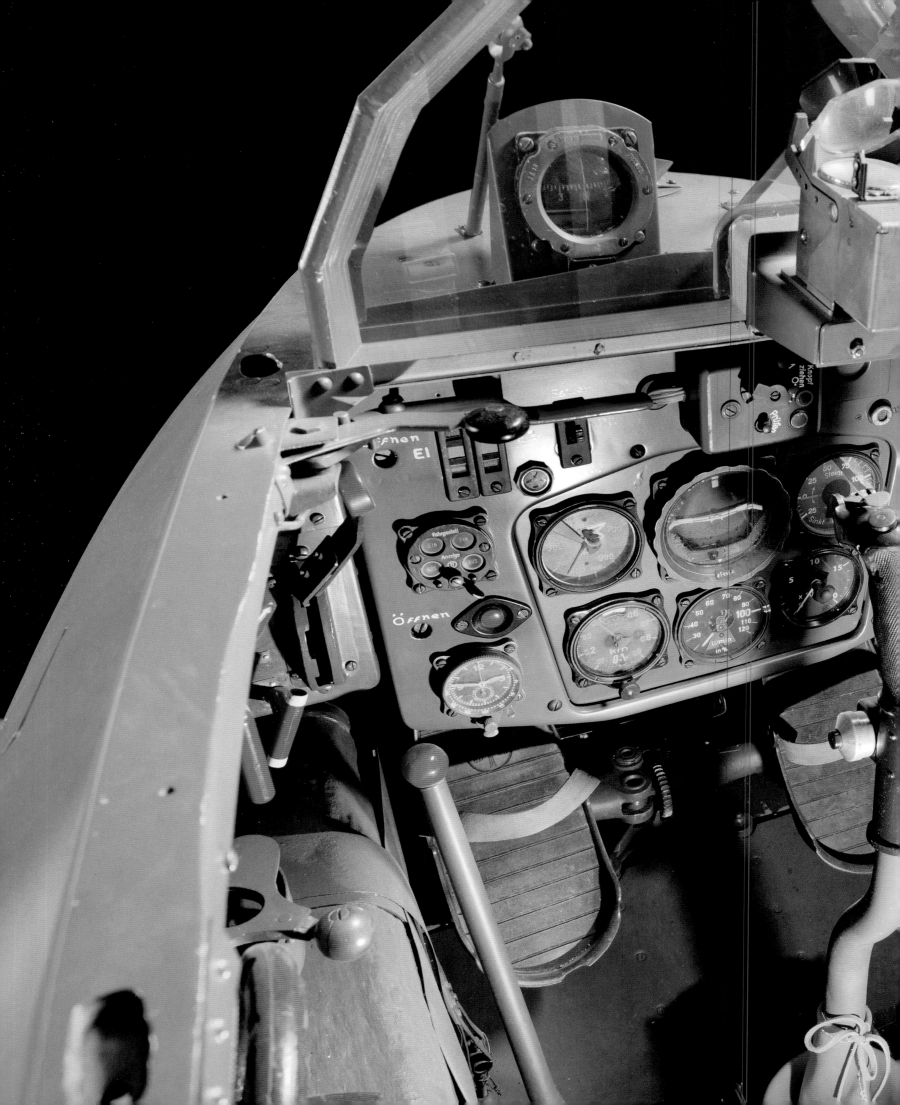

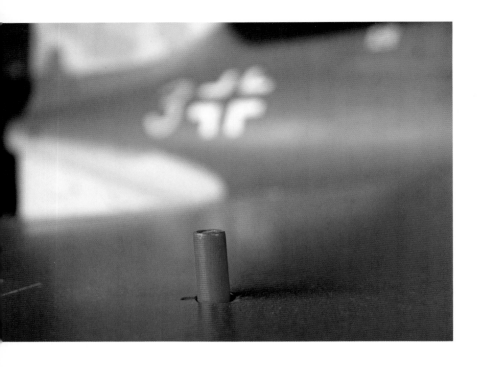

LEFT: Some aircraft have pins in the wings to indicate to the pilot when the landing gear is down. Since the Me 163 has no real landing gear, the red pins in the wings work to let the pilot know when the plane's flaps have been deployed.

BELOW: The pint-sized "propeller" at the front of the *Komet*'s armored nose is actually an impellor. When the fuel from the rocket fighter was used up, these spinning blades provided power to keep the *Komet*'s electrical system and instruments up and running until the plane touched down for landing. INSET: Simply screwing in fasteners as tight as you can "does not fly" on an operational aircraft. Nuts and bolts are safety-wired into place to keep them from working loose through vibration. These wires appear on the nose of the *Komet*'s impellor.

PREVIOUS PAGES: The *Komet*'s fuselage was bulbous on the outside and cramped on the inside. In an effort to get more fuel in the plane, there isn't too much room for the pilot. Note the huge, heavy, flat slab of 80-millimeter thick glass up front, designed to stop .50-caliber bullets from American bombers.

This RAE batch of aircraft accounts for many of the Me 163s preserved today in museums, including *Komets* at the Science Museum in London, US Air Force Museum in Ohio, Luftwaffe Museum in Berlin, Australian War Memorial in Canberra, and Canada Aviation Museum in Ottawa.

At the RAE facility, the aircraft were studied thoroughly, so that the technologies could be acquired for future military applications. At least one of the *Komets* was painted with RAF roundels and fin flash, and made a number of towed flights behind a Spitfire Mk.IX and glides until it was wrecked during a rough landing in 1947.

The FHC aircraft was assigned code AM 214 and given to the No. 6 Maintenance Unit. When that RAE unit moved to Brize Norton on July 26, 1945, the aircraft went, too. The aircraft was no longer considered a valuable war prize by September 1946 and was transferred to the Royal Air Force College, the RAF's training and education academy, at Cranwell. It was housed in the Station Museum on Cranwell North airfield.

The Me 163 was in this museum until 1961 when it was transferred to the Imperial War Museum (IWM) for exhibit. Here, it was displayed in the main museum building on Lambeth Road in London. Rumors are that the original wings were damaged and that parts of other *Komets* were used to make this plane whole again. It appears in photos from the era with heavily speckled brown and green topsides and the red numeral "3" on the tail. The emblem of the I./JG 400, Baron von Münchhausen happily riding a flying cannonball, graced the nose. The plane had most definitely been repainted since its German service, either at Cranwell or right after it arrived at the IWM.

Meanwhile, the IWM had been looking for a suitable site for the storage, restoration, and eventual display of exhibits that were too large for its headquarters in London. The organization obtained permission to use Duxford airfield for this purpose. Cambridgeshire County Council joined with the IWM and the Duxford Aviation Society and, in 1977, bought the runway to give the abandoned aerodrome a new lease of life.

The *Komet* was moved to Duxford before, or right after the facility opened. R. L. Bossom worked on the *Komet* when it was at Duxford and stated on a *Komet* website:

"When it arrived from Lambeth it was painted in four-inch paintbrush 'garden gate green' and brown and it was in a disheveled state. We were asked by the Director to 'tart it up' for display. We had to try and find out as much as possible

ABOVE: The FHC's Me 163 wears a strange symbol on its side—German Baron Münchhausen flying skyward on an uncorked bottle of champagne. In the famous story, notorious tall-tale-teller Münchhausen rides a cannonball, but the symbol of the .7/JG 400 was the Baron atop a hissing bottle of sparkling wine, a fitting emblem considering the *Komet*'s explosive liquid fuel.

about 191660 and this proved to be a mammoth task. The markings were not in the correct places, so we had to buy the books by Mano Ziegler and Jeffrey Ethell to try to find out more. The painting [of the *Komet* took place] over four years.

"We were promised a blown canopy but it never came. The damage to the bulletproof screen appeared in the hangar at Duxford, but I am not sure why. It cannot be proved, but it took a heavy landing at some time since the landing skid was misshapen. It may also have been due to ground handling. The cockpit instrument panel was refurbished in my kitchen, as all the wiring had been cut through from behind this panel after the war, so was easy to remove.

"All the time I worked on it I was amazed at the workmanship and quality of the design of the airframe."

In 1997, the *Komet* was moved to Duxford's restoration building—an area open to the public in which aircraft were

ABOVE: Like the Messerschmitt Bf 109, the Me 262 has leading edge slats that automatically deploy at slow speeds. On the ground, you can push the slats upward and aft, and they will fall back into place as soon as you let go. At cruising speed, the air passing over the wing holds the slats in place. When the plane slows, the slats thump down automatically.

refurbished by IWM staff and volunteers. During the restoration, a complete engine, canopy parts, and cannons were installed. The cockpit remained only partly complete.

In October 1997, Duxford's Messerschmitt Bf 109 G-2 suffered engine troubles during an airshow and crash-landed in a field. The plane flipped on its back and suffered major damage. Due to this accident, the spot in the restoration hangar assigned to the *Komet* was taken over by those working on the Bf 109 wreck.

The *Komet* was moved to a side building. Periodically, a tourist or enthusiast would sneak behind the museum's barriers and snap an image of the rocket plane, wings off, in a back corner of the facility. In May 2005, the *Komet* was loaded on a truck and taken away.

It was soon discovered that the aircraft was sold in order for the IWM to raise the money it needed to acquire one of two de Havilland D.H.9s found in an elephant stable in India. This aircraft was badly wanted by the museum because D.H.9s operated from Duxford during World War I. Correspondence between IWM trustees and the FHC date to late 2003. The FHC purchased the *Komet* in 2005.

In 2007, Vulcan entered into an agreement with Legend Flyers, based at Paine Field, to restore the *Komet*. The group was quite familiar with radical German aircraft, being involved in the work of creating five Me 262 replicas for aviation museums. The *Komet* went into restoration in November 2007 and was finished in April 2008. The craftsmen at Legend Flyers had assistance from Rudolf Reinhold Opitz, Gruppenkommandeur II./JG 400, on the Luftwaffe markings and nose art.

The newly restored *Komet* arrived on site before the June 2008 opening of the Paine Field building, and stands on static display at the southeast end of the hangar.

More impactful on the future of aviation technology than the Me 163 was Messerschmitt's Me 262 jet fighter. Nearly every modern jet aircraft in the world owes some of its traits, characteristics, and design elements to this iconic fighter aircraft of World War II.

The fighter got its start in 1938 when the German Air Ministry approached Messerschmitt about making an airframe for new jet engines under development at Junkers and BMW. Many in the Luftwaffe considered these new engines to be the key to the next generation of combat aircraft.

However, constant delays and production problems plagued the construction of these jet engines. BMW and

ABOVE: With unpainted engine inlet cowlings, the FHC's Me 262 was photographed in France at the end of World War II. The plane still has its original nose in this image, complete with bulges for aerial camera equipment.

Junkers were forced to redesign their complex power plants many times. While waiting to get viable engines from BMW, Messerschmitt chose to fly the aircraft with a piston-powered Jumo 210 engine mounted in the nose.

The propeller-driven Me 262 took to the skies for the first time in April 1941. Soon, BMW released early versions of their jet engines to Messerschmitt, but both engines failed during the Me 262's first jet-powered takeoff in November 1941.

While still waiting for dependable power, Messerschmitt redesigned the plane. After each failure, it seemed, the promised jet engines got bigger and heavier, and were predicted to produce less thrust. In order to compensate for more weight and keep the Me 262 suitably balanced, Messerschmitt ordered the outer wings of the aircraft to be swept aft. The rushed design change was purely the simplest solution to a complex problem, but it ultimately helped the fighter's performance. The swept-back wings helped delay the onset of high-speed buffeting and compressibility, making the plane capable of high subsonic speeds.

Luftwaffe test pilots were quite pleased with the radical jet fighter, but Hitler seemed fixated on making the Me 262 a bomber. While Messerschmitt worked to incorporate conversions to allow the plane fly with a bombsight, additional fuel, and a meager load of explosives, precious months slipped away.

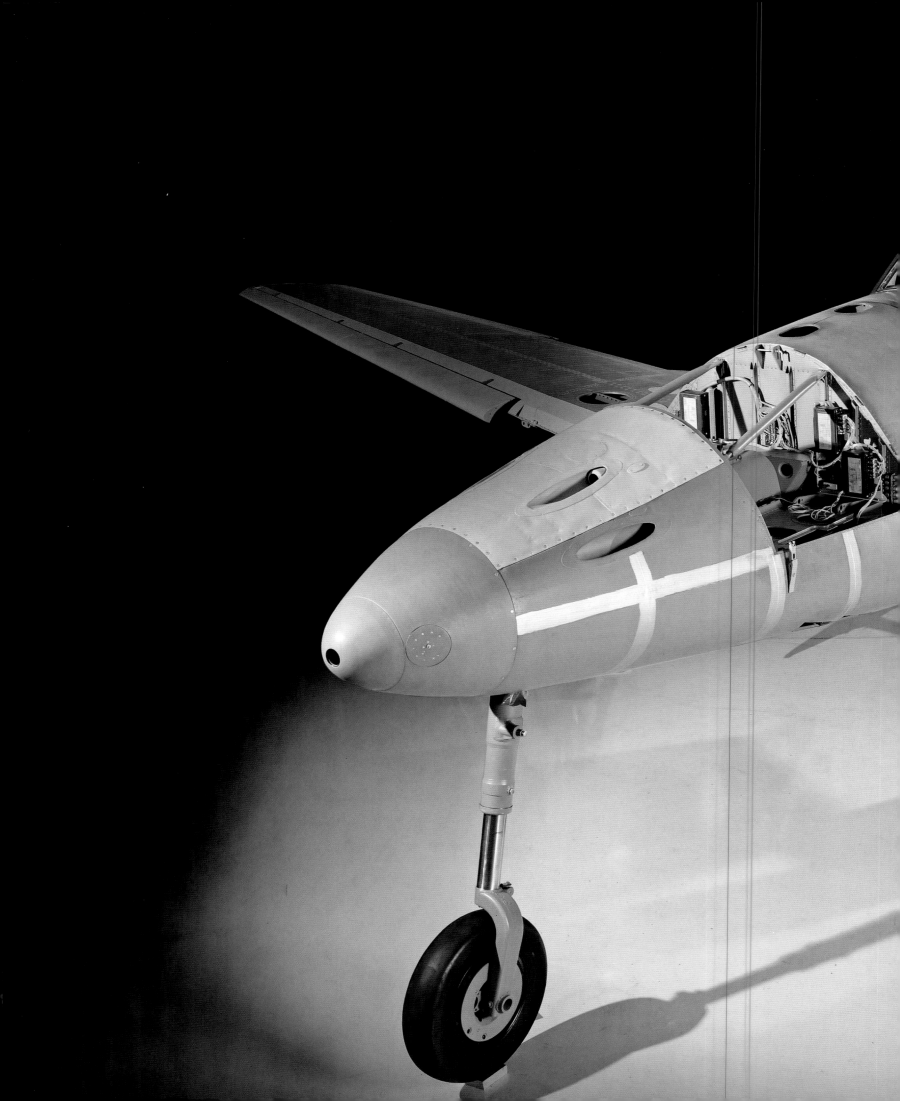

LEFT: Shot at an engine shop in California, the first of the Me 262's Jumo 004 engines takes shape. By using improved metals and modern techniques, engineers hope to get hundreds of hours out of the engines before overhaul.

PREVIOUS PAGES: The FHC's Messerschmitt Me 262 has a storied history; with the Luftwaffe, the US Army Air Forces, and Howard Hughes's RKO Pictures. It is now being restored to take to the skies once again.

By mid-1944, after more painful delays caused by German leadership decisions and the difficulties of producing a sophisticated aircraft with its industry in tatters, Messerschmitt Me 262s began to be built in numbers. Combat versions of the plane flew with Junkers Jumo 004 jet engines, instead of those from BMW, producing over 1,900 pounds of thrust each.

Despite compromises with engines and airframe, the Me 262 was an amazing aircraft—able to outpace the Allied fighters by 120 mph or more. The four 30mm MK 108s cannon in its nose made it deadly when attacking American heavy bombers.

Though the airframe of the Me 262 was fairly conventional, the Jumo 004 jet engines made the plane tricky to fly. The Jumos were far from perfect, though better than the early BMW engines. A pilot had to use great care, because quick throttle movements could cause compressor stalls. While a stall was something a flyer could recover from, too much power too quickly would burn out critical components housed in the "hot section" of the engine, destroying the Jumo 004 in flight.

The Jumo engine compressor blade wheels were made with weaker metals, prone to failure, because many high-quality metals were going to the production of German submarines. Other parts of the power plant, exposed to great heat, should have been made of high-quality metals but were instead made from mild steel parts coated aluminum. As a result, the life of a Jumo 004 engine in combat was less than twenty-five hours.

Ultimately, it was Germany's dire situation that doomed the Messerschmitt Me 262. With weak parts, a shortage of fuel, and very few surviving experienced pilots, it did not matter that the Me 262 was a superior plane. Great numbers of conventional Allied aircraft were attacking Germany daily, and a handful of amazing Me 262 jet fighters piloted by a dwindling group of brave fighter pilots could do nothing to stop the decimation of Germany.

According to one source, the FHC Me 262 took to the air on March 14, 1945, with Messerschmitt factory pilot Otto Kaiser at the controls. This was at a flight test facility in Memmingen, Germany. Given the location of the flight, Leipheim and Burgau were the likely locations for the plane's final assembly in early March.

Very little is known about the Luftwaffe service history of this Me 262. American soldiers found the aircraft at an airfield near Lechfeld, south of Augsburg, Germany. The plane was found and photographed in A-1a/U3 configuration, meaning the plane had different nose hardware than the standard fighter-type Me 262. The 30mm guns were replaced with a pair of R6-50/30 vertical cameras in the nose compartment.

The large film boxes for the cameras protruded past the streamlined form of the nosecone necessitating the addition of two distinctive blisters on either side of the front of the aircraft nose. This U3 configuration modification was often completed during the war by Lufthansa at Eger-Cheb, Czechoslovakia.

At Lechfeld, the plane came under the jurisdiction of the 54th Air Disarmament Squadron (ADS) of the US Army. The German crosses on the sides of the plane were painted over with US insignia. The swastika at the tail was also painted over. The Me 262 received the moniker *Connie the Sharp Article*, inspired by the name of the wife of ADS Master Sgt. H. L. Preston.

Later, as the plane was being prepared for ferrying to a port France, it was renamed *Pick II* by its adopted pilot, Lt. Roy Brown of the 86th Fighter Group. Brown's P-47, *Pick*, had been named after his wife whose maiden name was Pickrell. The Me 262 was also assigned the number 444 by the Air Technical Intelligence group.

The planes were flown from Lechfeld to the port of Cherbourg, France. By July 19, 1945, the Me 262 and forty other aircraft, including the FHC Fw 190 D-13, were loaded aboard the British escort carrier HMS *Reaper*.

At a port near Newark, New Jersey, the group of aircraft was divided. Some went to the navy, while others were bound for the army's Wright Field in Ohio. Still others, under the army's jurisdiction, were diverted to Freeman Field in Seymour, Indiana, "when the field (Wright) could no longer handle additional aircraft." Colonel Harold E. Watson, the leader of the "Watson's Whizzers" evaluation group, flew *Pick II* accompanied by another 262 flown by a pilot named Jim Holt. Both pilots experienced difficulties with the brakes on their jets during a fuel stop in Pittsburg. Watson managed to stop *Pick II*, while Holt's aircraft crashed off the end of the runway. The

continued on page 236

BELOW: A milestone in the restoration of the FHC's Me 262 took place when its one-piece wing was joined to the jet fighter's fuselage. The wing is held in place by four large bolts. When the plane is taken to an isolated airfield for test flights, crews will have to disassemble the body and wings once again.

FOLLOWING PAGES: The big gun bay of the Me 262 carried four Mk 108 30mm cannon. Eventually, demilitarized examples of the guns will be installed in the nose as the heavy cannon are critical to the weight and balance of the flying aircraft.

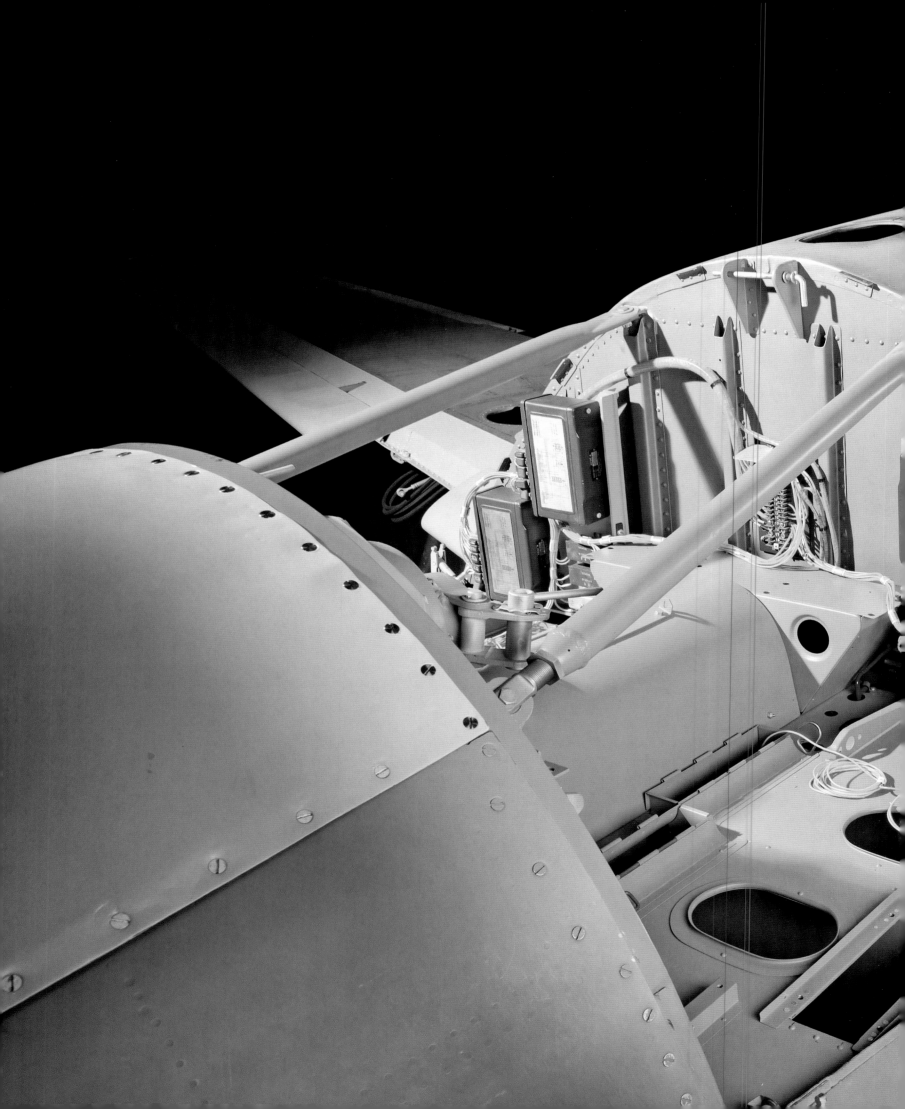

ABOVE: The Messerschmitt Me 262 has a shark-like appearance when viewed from the front. The flat lower fuselage acted as a lifting body for the heavy jet fighter. The lens in the very tip of the Messerschmitt's long nose is for the plane's gun camera.

OPPOSITE: This image shows the half-built cockpit of the FHC's Messerschmitt Me 262. It was here that Colonel Watson, of "Watson's Whizzers" fame, sat as he flew this aircraft to Ohio. Renowned German ace Adolph Galland took a turn in the pilot's seat when the plane was on display at Planes of Fame. And, most likely, Howard Hughes, too, sat in the cockpit of this famous jet fighter.

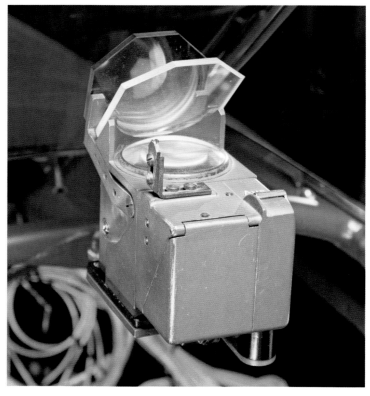

TOP: An early Allied drawing shows the strange plane, without propellers, that the flyers were encountering over Europe. The artist got most of the traits of the Me 262 right, though out of habit perhaps, he could not help but depict the plane with almost completely straight wings.

ABOVE: Replacing the plane's thick glass windscreen was a challenge for restorers. The unit is almost three inches thick, and yet nearly distortion free. The plane's gunsight can be rotated clockwise and pushed forward to get it out of the way when not in use.

continued from page 231

other Me 262 was destroyed, but Holt walked away from the crash. Soon after, Watson piloted *Pick II* to Freeman Field. There, the plane was assigned the designator "FE-4012." At Freeman, the Me 262 was equipped with a fighter-style nose from another Me 262, designated FE-111. The latter plane is today on display at the Smithsonian National Air and Space Museum in Washington, D.C.

FE-4012, the FHC aircraft, was reconditioned at Freeman Field and given an overall smooth finish for performance comparison testing with the American Lockheed P-80 Shooting Star jet fighter. On about May 17, 1946, Watson flew the aircraft to Patterson Field for the start of this series of trials. It was flown at Patterson and Wright Fields on test work for four hours and forty minutes spread over eight flights. Flight trials were discontinued in August 1946 after four engine changes were required during the course of the tests culminating in two single-engine landings.

Now, no longer of use to the army, it was handed over to the Hughes Aircraft Company of Culver City, California. It is rumored that Howard Hughes himself was interested in the aircraft for more than technical study. Many sources state that Hughes intended to enter the aircraft in the post-war Thompson Trophy air race, but top generals are said to have "discouraged" Hughes. The US military was going to enter a P-80 Shooting Star jet fighter in the race and it would make for bad press should a German design win the high-speed dash instead of the hometown, or homeland, favorite. The plane's engines were run at the Culver City plant, but it was never flown. About this time, the FE-4012 number was changed to T2-4012.

RKO Pictures, a Hughes-controlled movie studio, asked to use the jet as a prop in a film in 1949. The air force agreed and the plane was transported from the Hughes Aircraft Company to an RKO lot. The plane remained with the studio for two years and appeared in early versions of the John Wayne film that would become *Jet Pilot* some eight years later.

RKO attempted to return 4012 to the air force in 1951, but it was no longer wanted. Since donation was easier than scrapping the plane, it was given to Glendale Aeronautical School for use by students as an instructional airframe.

Edward T. Maloney acquired the plane, now in fairly rough shape, in approximately 1955 for his Planes of Fame Air Museum, then at Claremont, California. The plane stayed in the museum collection for many years and underwent one or more restorations. It was marked in a "White Nine" color scheme copied from another long lost 262.

In 2000, the FHC purchased the Me 262 and another aircraft from Edward Maloney. The restoration of this rare airframe was taken on by a number of companies—JME Aviation Ltd. in England, GossHawk Unlimited Inc. in Arizona, and Morgan Aircraft Restorations in Washington.

Aero Turbine Inc. in California tackled perhaps the most challenging part of the restoration. Two wartime Jumo 004 jet engines are currently being rebuilt using modern metals in critical spots to extend the life of the engines to several hundred hours of flight time.

When the Me 262 flies for the first time since World War II, it will be the only original, flying Messerschmitt Me 262 in the world.

TOP: American soldiers swarm over an abandoned Me 262 they found hidden among the trees near the front lines. In the last months of the war, German aviation units often dispersed their planes in the woods, flying from sections of the *Autobahn* to avoid Allied fighter bombers prowling the German airfields.

ABOVE: The FHC's Messerschmitt, smoothed for speed tests, was photographed at Wright Field during evaluations. Tests on the plane ceased after a series of engine failures similar to those experienced while the Me 262 jet fighter was used in combat by the Germans.

RIGHT: The fuel tank access doors on the belly of the aircraft are made from a primitive sort of honeycomb structure. The spot-welded steel grid is sandwiched between two steel sheets. Built near the end of the war, the Germans were often forced to use steel in the place of lighter aluminum alloys.

ABOUT THE AUTHOR

Cory Graff has over eighteen years' experience working in aviation museums, creating exhibits, conducting historical research, and educating visitors. He is the Flying Heritage Collection's Military Aviation Curator. In the past, Graff has worked at The Museum of Flight in Seattle, Washington and collaborated with the Whatcom Museum of History and Art, the Frye Art Museum, the Washington State History Museum, the Puget Sound Navy Museum, and the Museum of Glass. Graff is the author of eight books on various aviation and military history subjects. He has also co-created four additional books with museums and private publishers. He has written for *Air & Space Smithsonian*, *Air Classics*, *Aloft Magazine*, and *Warbirds International*.

ACKNOWLEDGMENTS

No book is created by one person alone. I would like to thank the following individuals and institutions for their contributions to this volume: Katherine Williams, Amy Heidrick, John Little, and P. J. Müller at The Museum of Flight, Miles Harris, P. Janine Kennedy, Calvin Graff, Owen Richards, "Bud" Tordoff, Ralph Jenkins, Erik Gilg, Tracy Stanley, and the staff at the National Archives and Records Administration, and Jason Fortenbacher of Fight to Fly Photography.

Special thanks to Jim Larsen and Heath Moffatt, who donated so many of their wonderful images of FHC aircraft and artifacts to this project. And thanks to Todd Shaphren, who helped research and write many of the FHC's aircraft histories used in this book. Finally, a big thanks to the staff, pilots, and volunteers at the FHC. Without them, this book would have never been written.

PHOTO CREDITS

INDEX